SIMONE de BEAUVOIR

SIMONE de BEAUVOIR

A feminist mandarin

Mary Evans

Tavistock
London and New York

First published in 1985 by
Tavistock Publications Ltd
11 New Fetter Lane,
London EC4P 4EE

Published in the USA by
Tavistock Publications in
association with Methuen, Inc.
733 Third Avenue, New York,
NY 10017

Typeset in Great Britain by Keyset
Composition, Colchester, Essex
Printed in Great Britain by
Richard Clay, The Chaucer Press,
Bungay, Suffolk

*British Library Cataloguing in
Publication Data*
Evans, Mary, *1946–*
    Simone de Beauvoir : a feminist
    mandarin.
    (Social science paperback; 294)
    1. Beauvoir, Simone de
    2. Women—Social
    conditions
    I. Title   II. Series
    305.4'2'0924   HQ1121
    ISBN 0–422–79510–0

*Library of Congress Cataloging in
Publication Data*
Evans, Mary, 1946–
    Simone de Beauvoir, a feminist
    mandarin.
    (Social science paperbacks ; 294)
    Bibliography: p.
    Includes index.
    1. Beauvoir, Simone de, 1908–
        —Political and social views.
    2. Feminism and literature—
    France.   I. Title.   II. Series.
    PQ2603.E362Z665   1985
    848'.91409   85–2647
    ISBN 0–422–79510–0 (pbk.)

Contents

Abbreviations used in the text

The following abbreviations of titles have been used:

MDD	*Memoirs of a Dutiful Daughter*
VED	*A Very Easy Death*
PL	*The Prime of Life*
SS	*The Second Sex*
FC	*Force of Circumstance*
ES	*Entretiens avec Jean-Paul Sartre, août-septembre 1974*
SCS	*She Came to Stay*
EA	*The Ethics of Ambiguity*
TM	*The Mandarins*
ASD	*All Said and Done*
BI	*Les Belles Images*
BB	*Brigitte Bardot and the Lolita Syndrome*
OA	*Old Age*
WTS	*When Things of the Spirit Come First*
LC	*Lettres au Castor et à quelques autres*
CA	*La Cérémonie des adieux*

These are listed in the order in which they appear. Full details of all titles are given in the Bibliography.

_____Acknowledgements_____

During the years that I spent writing this book I discussed many of the issues involved with a number of people. I would like to record my gratitude to all of them for their time, their help, and the constant sense of their friendship and support. My thanks, therefore, to Anne Seller, Clare Ungerson, Gaye Tuchman, Gill Davies, Janet Montefiore, Janet Sayers, Jeffrey Weeks, Joyce Rock, Kate McLuskie, Kathy Barry, Pat Macpherson, Nancy Black, Roisin Battel, and Val Hey. I also want to thank Yvonne Latham and Sue Macdonald for their help in typing, and re-typing, the manuscript and the staff of the library at the University of Kent at Canterbury for their assistance. To David Morgan I owe a particular debt of gratitude for the many hours that he has spent reading and discussing this essay: many of the central arguments involved have been formed and clarified in the course of those discussions.

_____Introduction_____

One of the central tenets of contemporary feminism is that is is a non-hierarchical and democratic movement. Yet like any social movement it numbers some who are more articulate and more literate than others. Of that number Simone de Beauvoir ranks as both outstandingly articulate and literate, and for contemporary feminism the life and work of Simone de Beauvoir have a central importance. De Beauvoir's *The Second Sex* is widely regarded as the major feminist text of the twentieth century and de Beauvoir's life, as an autonomous and self-defining woman of letters, is often seen as an inspiration to others. Her early commitment to literature has lasted throughout her life and, whatever the stresses and vicissitudes of her personal history, that central, literary theme runs consistently through her life. Indeed, de Beauvoir herself acknowledges that writing has given her more pleasure than any other event or activity. And her life has not been confined or uneventful: with her friend and companion Jean-Paul Sartre, she shared a life rich in the experience of travel, intellectual activity, and a cosmopolitan network of friends. Such a life was possible because de Beauvoir did not experience any of the constraints traditionally experienced by the majority of women writers. She did not write in the odd cracks of life free from domestic duties or the care of children nor did she have to strive – like many of both sexes – for education and access to the academic and literary world. Her own background was sufficiently privileged for higher education to be available – even for a girl in France in the 1920s – and although de Beauvoir has often been poor her poverty has been of a temporary kind. De Beauvoir, therefore, has not shared two of the characteristics of the majority of the women (and indeed the people) of the world – she has been neither a parent, nor poor. On the other hand, unlike many who are neither poor nor parents, de Beauvoir has consistently challenged the taken-for-granted attitudes of western bourgeois society, and remained an active critic of the society she inhabits. Her association with feminism took some years to emerge; what long pre-dates this is a commitment to, and identification with, left-wing and radical politics.

So de Beauvoir has used her pen to question accepted values and customs. She has lived outside conventional bourgeois society, refused honours, and chosen on certain occasions to place herself in situations involving personal danger and vilification. For example, she chose to oppose French policies in Algeria, and in doing so ran the risk of physical attack. While her life has been largely that of literature, it has also been that of a person who is much engaged with immediate and contentious social events. Small wonder, then, that contemporary feminism should find so much to respect and admire in this woman. In a culture which does not accept criticism easily, least of all from a woman who identifies with the left, she provides an outstanding example of a life of honest and disinterested scepticism and dissent. Whatever the other problems inherent in her work, opportunism is not amongst them.

But the high degree of respect which is due to de Beauvoir does not mean that her work should be exempt from discussion and criticism. Indeed, it is precisely because de Beauvoir occupies such a central place in the history of feminism that her work demands critical attention, in terms both of the work itself and of the issues and problems that it raises for feminism. Although she herself has recently suggested that too much attention has been paid to her writing on women, and too little to other aspects of her work, it is probably for her monumental study of women, *The Second Sex,* that de Beauvoir will be remembered. In the history of feminism no other work approaches either the range or the scope of that study. Yet as de Beauvoir has pointed out, it is only one of her many books, and was not written as part of a self-consciously feminist stance. *The Second Sex* was published in 1949; the conscious engagement with feminism came later, for it was not till the early 1970s that de Beauvoir became involved with active feminist politics, and was, in a sense, co-opted into a movement which she had – by both inspiration and example – helped to establish.

But until the 1970s there was, in France, little active feminism for de Beauvoir to engage with. There were, in France just as in other societies, those semi-public networks and associations of women which existed specifically to help and further women's interests, but active feminism – in the sense of an organized movement committed to structural change in the situation of women – was notably absent from France.[1] The politics in which de Beauvoir was involved prior to her involvement with feminism was the formal, traditional politics dominated by men: politics about government and the state, the politics of a public world from which women were largely excluded. Thus in writing (either *The Second Sex* or other of her works) de Beauvoir's experiences was that of a woman writing about women, but as a woman educated by, and with, men, a woman who largely associated with men and lived what could be described as a 'bachelor existence'. It is this aspect of de Beauvoir's life that provides one of the central themes of this study – how the feminism of this extraordinary and gifted woman was shaped by the very patriarchal values and habits that her later followers would question and condemn. Now that de Beauvoir is identified as one of the founding members of western feminism, it is almost heretical to ask whether or not she actually has claims to be called a feminist, but this issue raises questions about what feminism stands for, and who can properly be described as a feminist. It is surely no longer the case that all strong-minded, or determined, or successful women can be called feminists. If they could, then Mrs Thatcher, Simone de Beauvoir, and Barbara Cartland could all be included in the same category.

So the problem of defining feminism and feminists constitutes a second theme of this study. I wish to suggest that although it has sometimes been construed as such, feminism is not merely 'woman-centredness'. Equally, as Rosalind Coward[2] has persuasively argued, writing about women does not constitute feminism. In the context of de Beauvoir's own novels, for example, I shall argue that there is little to suggest that the novels were written by a feminist, or even by a woman. One might detect, in de Beauvoir's fiction, that the author is French, a socialist, and a philosopher, but there is little to identify the author as a feminist. Indeed, if de Beauvoir had not written *The Second Sex*, it is not inconceivable that she would never have been identified with feminism at all. It is true that she may well have given her support to causes such as the liberalization of the French abortion laws, but then so did many other women, and men, who had no significant or specific commitment to or identification with feminism.

But if feminism is not merely about 'woman-centredness' then the question has to be asked, and – even more difficult – answered, of exactly what it is. It is not enough to say that feminism involves a critical re-evaluation of the current social position of women in the west since criticism of the contemporary role and status of women could imply views that sanction the return to a more traditional role as much as the argument for their greater emancipation. Again, the use of terms such as 'emancipation' raises problems of definition. To suppose, for example, that the emancipation of women involves the entry of women into paid work has long been questioned by feminists. They point out that if women enter paid work then they all too often take on another job besides the one they already have – namely the care of dependent men and children. All available evidence points to the lasting strength of the sexual division of labour in the household and its apparent complete resistance to changes in society as a whole.

De Beauvoir's answer to 'the woman question' was the adoption by women of male habits and values. She counselled women against motherhood, advocated economic independence, and praised emotional autonomy. In this she followed that tradition within feminism which has always advocated the rejection of conventional femininity – the tradition which fought for access to the professions, higher education, and control over property. Basing her analysis on existentialist principles and values, de Beauvoir argued that women should reject their subordination and take their places in the public world of men as autonomous individuals. Unlike later feminists, who have placed great emphasis on the traditional role of women and lauded as essentially positive and valuable the care and nurture provided by women, de Beauvoir has questioned the ties to others that have bound women to men and children. It is true that de Beauvoir has assumed the subordination of women – perhaps a *sine qua non* for a feminist – but on the other hand she offers to contemporary feminism a confusing message: reject subordination as a woman by rejecting traditional femininity and taking on male assumptions and values.

But this statement about de Beauvoir implies that contemporary feminism has homogeneous objectives and principles. That this is not the case has been demonstrated, both in practice and in print. There are certainly issues on which women unite, but at the same time if these issues are examined it is apparent there is no necessary reason why commitment to that particular position should be identified with feminism. For example, to demand unrestricted access to contra-ception and abortion is often as much in the interests of men as women, and recent polemics on pornography have demonstrated that while some feminists regard pornography as evil and degrading to women others have suggested an underlying prurience in the attitudes to sexuality that are involved in the condemnation of pornography. The latter debate has in fact highlighted both specific and general underlying assumptions in feminism, and questioned the taken-for-granted validity of what has passed for feminist orthodoxy on pornography and sexual practice.[3]

Hence in a number of ways feminism can be 'deconstructed' so that what emerges at the end of the day is at best a loose federation of women with different interests and diverse moral and political values. All groups agree that women are subordinate to men, but again the implications – and indeed the very definition of this position – are numerous. To say that women are subordinate to men implies a generality of experience among women that is questionable, not to mention the other generality – of superiority – that it implies among men. Indeed, if the concept of the subordination of women is examined critically it becomes apparent that the exact nature of women's subordination is often ill-defined. This is not to say that there are not clear and quite unambiguous examples of areas in which women experience explicit discrimination (for example, unequal pay for equal work); but it means that the very concept of subordination contains within it values that are closely related to the experiences and values of white, western middleclass men. Chief among the values to which this group subscribes are individualism, competition, and emotional autonomy – the kind of values that are irrelevant in societies and to people without meritocratic hierarchies, nuclear families, and a rigid separation between the public and private world. But the transformation in values that took place in Europe as a result of the Protestant Reformation and the development of a market economy established what has been described as the 'theory of possessive individualism' as the central value of western society. Since societies do not change or develop in tidy and uniform ways, some groups within western society have not embraced with wholehearted enthusiasm the values of Samuel Smiles and the thrusting entrepreneur. Among those who have, for various reasons and to various degrees, maintained and articulated alternative values are the working class, and women. The working class in industrial capitalism has been forced to develop alternatives to individualism and competitiveness: the history of the western working class since the eighteenth century has been about the establishment of values of solidarity and co-operation. These values arise from the working-class experience of work: workers have had to fight for each and every concession from their employers, a fight which could not be conducted on an individual basis.

Just as the working class has maintained a set of alternative values, so too, in different ways and for different reasons, have women. Again, these values, of nurturing and personal care, have not arisen out of thin air, but out of the material experiences of the majority of women – experiences which include the care of children and other dependants. This is not to say that women have self-consciously set themselves up as the maintainers of moral and social standards, although this has on occasion been the case, but that the logic of social development, rather than personal choice, has assigned to women the responsibility for child care and generalized nurturing. Nor does the assertion that women have been the nurturant sex imply that men have not, albeit with wide variations, maintained, supported, and cared for their families and dependants. But the crucial difference between the experience of the sexes (whatever their class position) has been the relative independence of men set against the dependence of women. In a society which values independence, and is generally at odds with the idea of interdependence (since this implies precisely the kind of ties of solidarity so much vilified by critics of trade unions or working-class associations), it is scarcely surprising that for some women the idea and/or the experience of dependence on another is unacceptable, particularly – and crucially – given the ideology of patriarchal control within the family. Material dependence is one thing, social and emotional subservience as a result of that dependence is quite another.

Inevitably, therefore, the present organization and rationalization of family life (God created two sexes so that women could care for children, as Conservative cabinet ministers explain the sexual division of labour) are unacceptable: the contradiction between society's stress on individualism and independence in the case of men and dependence for women is too great. From the recognition of this contradiction comes the impetus for one tradition of feminism: women's assertion of their right to fulfil the very values society lauds for men. Within this tradition – within which de Beauvoir's work can be located – lie the concepts of equal opportunities and the formal emancipation of women into the public worlds of political control, meritocratic competition, and symbolic reward. (It is interesting to note here that when de Beauvoir and Sartre attempted to help young people – for example Lise and Olga of *The Prime of Life* – they did so in terms of encouraging their entry into the world of scholarship. Both Lise and Olga later took quite different paths.)

But at odds with this tradition is the tradition of interdependence and solidarity between women. This interdependence has taken many forms that are closely related to the different class positions of the women involved: middle-class women have united, generally in formal organizations, to demand access to higher education, enfranchisement, and other civil liberties. Working-class women have, both formally and informally, organized in trade unions and community-based associations. All these activities have in common the commitment to meet the specific needs of women; what separates the activities are the groups against whom the associations of women are organized and the values inherent in the campaign. For example, when middle-class women campaigned for higher education they campaigned to enter and maintain hierarchies with unequal reward structures, hierarchies which themselves could act against the interests of working-class women.

This tradition of bourgeois feminism has, to its eternal credit, fought and won victories – for example, over access to contraception – which have been of value to all women. But it is a tradition essentially about the amelioration of western society: it does not challenge the political economy of the west. Nor, I would argue, does the tradition within feminism which is based on the veneration of the traditional role of women – that is, the caring and nurturing woman. In part, of course, this caring and nurturing woman is a myth maintained by upholders of the status quo to *éncourager les autres* – or at least make them feel guilty if they do not fulfil its premises. Even so, feminists in the United States have recently argued for the politics of 'maternal thinking' and hence accepted the implicit belief that all mothers are good mothers and always act in the best interests of their children.[4] Certainly, the majority of mothers do a great deal of work for their children, but the feelings that accompany this hard work might on occasion be closer to the grudging, resentful, and hostile feeling that many employees feel for their bosses. The point avoided by the 'maternal thinkers' is that women are assigned the role of mother, but the interpretation of the role is varied and individual. To assume a uniform interpretation of the role, and to assume that it is always positive, is both to fly in the face of available evidence, and to trap women even further in the role of mother by praising what women do as mothers rather than stressing what men do not do as fathers. As all western societies face ever-rising rates of unemployment and increasing costs for the provision of state welfare benefits, the politics of 'maternal thinking', and the veneration of women's nurturing role, serve those interests in society which have much to gain by removing women from the work-force and encouraging them to act as a voluntary and unpaid extension of the welfare state.

So neither bourgeois feminism nor the politics of maternal thinking offers to western society any fundamental challenge. Again, it has to be reiterated that the changes advocated by both groups would bring about substantial and significant improvements for many. But the point here is that the changes would take place in the context of western, industrial capitalism. And that context is far more than the scenery against which we act out our lives: it is a form of social organization which structures and defines our lives. Men, Marx once wrote, make their own history, but they do so against the history and experiences of past ages. What has been said about men also applies to women, and it is this historical aspect of the context in which we live and act that is crucial for an understanding of both feminism and de Beauvoir's work. As suggested earlier, feminism did not invent many of its aims and values: they already existed, and their origin can be located within specific social and material relationships. The values of self-help, independence, the good mother, are not, therefore, ideas which appear out of nowhere; they are the rationalizations, the legitimations, and the explanations of particular forms that the satisfaction of human needs takes in our society.

Given that ideas are not produced out of nowhere but by specific experiences within specific contexts, it is essential in any study either of feminism as a whole or of one feminist in particular to engage with the relevant ideas in terms of their place in the social world as a whole. In the case of de Beauvoir's own work this sense of location and definition is largely absent, and absent in two ways which are crucial. First, de Beauvoir takes for granted a great deal about western bourgeois culture that feminists, of whatever persuasion, might now question. Second, her programmatic statements – whether about women or other political issues – are frequently made without reference to the context in which those issues arise. The majority of the commitments that de Beauvoir made, and makes, are faultlessly progressive. The problem is not, therefore, that de Beauvoir is on the 'wrong' side, in the sense of being reactionary or right wing, but that she offers a view of politics that is essentially idealist, in the sense of lacking a basis for the understanding of the derivation and location of political, social, and personal choices. Admittedly, as will be discussed later in this study, de Beauvoir accounts for the subordination of women outlined in *The Second Sex* by arguing that it is women's biology which condemns them to dependence, a dependence further enforced by the construction by men of female inferiority, but at the same time she does not include in her model of social relations any consideration of motives other than a male will to dominate women.

Such a view of relations between the sexes may, of course, be sufficient for some feminists. However, this study is written from the explicit view that the subordination of women (a subordination that is understood to be highly variable, both between and within societies, but essentially entails differences between men and women in the degree of power and control they can exercise over material and social resources) is not derived simply from the decision of men either as individuals or as collectivities to dominate, and maintain the domination of, women. The main enemy is not men, but neither is there any single main enemy. A good deal of ink has now been spilt on the question of the origins of the subordination of women: do they lie in capitalism? or in patriarchy? or in a bit of both? I shall argue here first that the subordination of women is so variable that a concept of universal subordination is often of as little analytical use as a concept of universal weather: the fact that it exists everywhere tells us little or nothing of any use about its specific forms. Thus de Beauvoir, in bequeathing to feminism a book which both deals with men and women in general terms, and posits a model of the universal and general subordination of women, provides feminism with a potentially dangerous and limiting basis for later politics. Certainly, *The Second Sex* and de Beauvoir's own brave outspokenness inspire, but the question here is whether or not that inspiration is enough, particularly as a basis for specific forms of political action.

So the second object of this essay is to examine, perhaps a little more critically than hitherto, the values implicit in de Beauvoir's work. They are, I wish to suggest, precisely the values – of independence, autonomy, and self-realization – that have done much to produce the very subordination of women that de Beauvoir attacks. That the values have also been responsible for aggressive imperialism, the massive exploitation of labour and natural resources, and individual self-aggrandisement must also be stated. But these values are not, as some recent feminist political activists have suggested, derived from a person's biology. The peace women's slogan 'take the toys from the boys' suggests precisely that identification of men with aggression and greed that I would not accept. Indeed, a theme of this essay is the inadequacy of essentialist explanations of male and female behaviour. It is of course the case that some men, although perhaps rather fewer than is sometimes argued, act in precisely those ways which conform to radical feminist stereotypes of the male sex. Men have waged war, subjected whole populations to want and poverty, and destroyed human associations and cultures. But these acts of gross violence have been directed as much against other men as against women, and the motives involved have been far more complicated than the simple desire to demonstrate male strength. Indeed, when the idea of male strength is deconstructed, it becomes apparent that our western ideas of 'strength' relate to indices of social or material power which are of less importance in other societies.

But the aspect of male power which seems to have had the greatest attraction for de Beauvoir is that of the intellect. Further, as her memoirs make apparent, integration into and participation in the world of intellectual and academic work was of paramount importance. Psychoanalysts would no doubt see this in terms of de Beauvoir's desire to make good the symbolic mutilation which as a woman she had inevitably suffered. Certainly, de Beauvoir's emphasis on the mind, on rational, structured thought, seems to be powered by a fierce determination to escape from the primitive chaos and disordered subjectivity of the world of women. The personal, emotional, problems which this juxtaposition of men with culture, and women with nature, raises for de Beauvoir will be discussed later; suffice to say here that throughout de Beauvoir's work there runs the theme of the danger of emotional life, particularly for women. The essential danger which she identifies is that women may direct all their emotional energies (and indeed all their energies) into relationships with men, who will then leave them, betray them, or become indifferent. But the answer which de Beauvoir provides to these dangers is for women to maintain an emotional independence and autonomy, and to control 'nature' by 'culture'.

The quarrel here, however, is not with the idea of the control of nature by culture, but with the reality and construction of the culture in question. In relation to de Beauvoir, and feminism, the issue therefore is how 'nature' is to be controlled: de Beauvoir largely opted for the extension of existing habits and assumptions to women; later feminists have taken the opposite view and advocated an almost wholesale rejection of existing culture precisely because it has been shaped in many important aspects by men. Both positions lead to their different absurdities: the veneration of intellectual order and logic, whatever their subject, and the veneration of instincts, whatever they are. But the fierce rejection by some feminists of systematized thought and organized politics is derived from a limited perception of the results such order has achieved, a perception that construes these results in negative terms. The alternative to this order is then described in terms of a return to nature and an assertion of natural powers and resources – terms which are familiar to any reader of western history since the industrial revolution, for there has always been a resistance in our culture, often justifiable given the forms which they have taken, to technology and technological control.

The occasional exaggerated hostility by groups within feminism to systems of thought and organization which leave little room for spontaneity should not, however, obscure the real problems for feminism which this issue raises: that of developing a political theory and practice which are neither a feminist version of romantic absurdities about nature (and in this case the view that nature is always a benign mother), nor are so arid that they appear to have little to do with human needs for affection, intimacy, and diversity. At this point in the history of feminism the need is particularly apparent: the feminism which draws its theoretical inspiration from Marxism can on occasion seem so Talmudic and its debates so scholastic that many become alienated from its politics; on the other hand, feminist politics of spontaneity, the veneration of a specific 'female-ness', and the rejection of heterosexuality are largely ineffective when faced with the realities of political power. The appeal of de Beauvoir's work is that she wrote of the individual needs, difficulties, and joys of women and men. The problem in her work, and one that remains of lasting interest to feminists, is her discussion of the reasons for individual choices and constraints. So in praising de Beauvoir, and declaring a commitment to socialism, this essay is designed to try and explore the ways in which de Beauvoir raised the issue of the relationship between the sexes and the nature of the analysis that she bequeathed to feminism.

1
_____Memoirs_____

When young, de Beauvoir stated her ambition was to 'construct a life that would be like no-one else's'. In this ambition she has largely succeeded, not least in the provision of five autobiographical works (*Memoirs of a Dutiful Daughter, The Prime of Life, Force of Circumstance, All Said and Done*, and *A Very Easy Death*) which provide considerable documentary information about the major events of her life. The richness of the life which she created for herself is amply demonstrated in her autobiography, a richness thrown into relief by the very simplicities of the essential structure of de Beauvoir's life: born in Paris, and determined from an early age to be a writer, she graduated in philosophy from the Sorbonne in 1929, taught in provincial *lycées* until 1938, returned to Paris, and, after the publication of *She Came to Stay* in 1943, devoted her life to writing. While a student she met Jean-Paul Sartre, with whom she was to remain 'firm friends' until his death in 1980.

But this summary of de Beauvoir's life does nothing like justice to many aspects of her emotional and intellectual career. Of particular interest here are two issues. First, how a girl from a conventional bourgeois home became a leading existentialist philosopher and writer and, later in her life, one of the major feminists of the twentieth century. The second question that arises from a study of her autobiography and her fiction is how far de Beauvoir, in rejecting the conventional role of women, substituted for it an existence which was nevertheless structured in its essential elements by male assumptions and needs. To assume that de Beauvoir constructed for herself what Carol Ascher has described as a 'life of freedom' (Ascher 1981) is to exaggerate certain unorthodox aspects of de Beauvoir's life at the cost of a consideration of the more conventional. In *The Second Sex* de Beauvoir was to write that 'women are made, not born', and she proceeded to reject, in a radical and innovative way, all theories which suggested the existence of something identifiable as a 'female' nature or a feminine personality. Yet to contemporary feminists this rejection of many traditional assumptions about women might in itself suggest oppression and over-determination by male-defined patterns, with the implication that women are allowed by patriarchal assumptions and ideologies to deviate from traditional femininity only by following a form of existence known to men.[1] The road that de Beauvoir chose, of commitment to intellectual life and the rejection of monogamy offered, and provided, numerous complexities of an interpersonal kind. De Beauvoir's inter-pretation of these difficulties, with its emphasis on individual differences and 'freely' made choices between particular men and women rather than on general differences between the sexes, now reads as a fascinating example of the individualization of experience. But as such it provides us with a vividly dramatized account of the difficulties which women and men face in trying to escape from the paths of bourgeois normality and traditional patterns of heterosexuality.

Nevertheless, to suppose that de Beauvoir established for herself, against all odds, a way of life previously unbeknown is a misinter-pretation of the essential elements of her life. Thus in considering both questions about de Beauvoir's biography it is important to stress the many factors in her background that must have encouraged as much as inhibited her progress towards an intellectual career, and economic and social independence. Nor should it be assumed too rapidly that the life which de Beauvoir chose for herself was one of insecurity and financial hardship: by the age of 23 she had qualified as a teacher of philosophy and was assured of an adequate income and considerable social status. In fact, in securing for herself professional and merito-cratic qualifications de Beauvoir had achieved the economic security she had known as a child, but had lost during adolescence when her father's fortunes had seriously declined. By her own efforts she had re-created the assured world which her father's dilettantism had lost.

The world into which de Beauvoir was born in 1908 was that of petit-bourgeois Paris: a world of comfort and affluence. The impression that de Beauvoir gives of these early years is one of warmth and physical delight, of the softness of her mother's body, the delightful, rich texture of hot chocolate, and the child's vivid enjoyment of sweet cakes and ices. But behind this apparent material ease and plenty there lurks an element of constant concern about money. As de Beauvoir notes, her family had to practise 'a genteel poverty', and after the First World War her father's fortunes took such a decided turn for the worse that the family was forced to move house: to leave the comfort and affluence of their flat in the Boulevard Raspail and take a new home in the Rue de Rennes. Moving house did not, for de Beauvoir, simply mean a change of physical location; it was much more significant as a social change and a decline in social status. Indeed, moving home marks the end of Book One of *Memoirs of a Dutiful Daughter*; this is not simply a change of address, but a change of life. From a secure position as the daughter of a prosperous lawyer, de Beauvoir now becomes the child of a man forced to work in a job provided by a relative's charity, a man increasingly embittered by the changes in the world and inadequate at dealing with them.

The decline in the fortunes of de Beauvoir's father becomes doubly dramatic for his daughter since it coincides with her adolescence. The contrast between Book One and Book Two is thus marked: in the first book a picture is drawn of a child who is very much at one with herself and her surroundings; in the second book the child has changed into an adolescent, living in some discomfort with both herself and her surroundings. Reconciliation between the self and the world begins in Book Three: in it de Beauvoir leaves the Cours Désir, the Catholic secondary school which she had hitherto attended, and enters the Institut Sainte-Marie, also a Catholic school, but one with some claim to academic competence. At last de Beauvoir finds elements of a world which she wishes to enter, one of serious intellectual work and open-mindedness to critical enquiry which had been altogether absent at the Cours Désir. But more than that, the Institut Sainte-Marie offered de Beauvoir a first glimpse of the possible existence of circumstances which could provide an integration of the self and the world: in thought and rationality one could become oneself.

In leaving the Cours Désir de Beauvoir left, however, more than just a school: she also turned her back on Catholicism and the influence of the religious beliefs and values of her mother. Within the de Beauvoir family there lay an absolute schism in terms of religious belief between mother and father: de Beauvoir's father had no such religious faith. Nevertheless, he made little attempt to challenge his wife's views, and seemed to accept that she should be able to pass on her values to her daughters. But religion never seems to have been an issue of active disagreement between de Beauvoir's parents; on that matter they had apparently agreed to disagree. Far more disruptive in terms of their own relationship was their increasing impoverishment, and the sourness and disenchantment that this created. Both father and mother came from wealthy families; de Beauvoir notes that her paternal grandfather inherited an estate of about 500 acres, and considerably enlarged his fortune on marriage. On both sides of her family de Beauvoir's world was one of familiarity with the ownership of property and its trappings – country estates, servants, dowries, and large houses.

The social relations that accompanied these material circumstances were organized by a strict code of manners and propriety. Social life revolved around the family and those privileged others known to be of *bonne famille*. Large-scale entertainments were undertaken at which considerable numbers of these socially suitable people met together to affirm their common identity and meet future marriage partners. Women were chaste until marriage, husbands held absolute authority in the family, and young people gave their parents complete obedience. As such, the French bourgeois family life which de Beauvoir knew was similar in its essential aspects to bourgeois family life in other European societies.

But of course the outward appearance of bourgeois normality had its other side. Three features of de Beauvoir's particular history seem to have led her to challenge the fabric and structure of her social world. First, the relative poverty of the de Beauvoir family made it impossible for them to play any real part in bourgeois social life. There was no money for entertaining, or attractive clothes, or the acts of apparent spontaneous generosity that support bourgeois entertaining's claim to originality and liveliness. Deprived of the material means to fulfil bourgeois expectations the de Beauvoirs had to fall back, like so many penniless bourgeois and petit bourgeois everywhere, on exaggerated adherence to the forms of bourgeois life. Thus it became a matter of pride for de Beauvoir's mother to reject extravagance or expensive tastes. Like a whole section of the English middle class, who have been so well portrayed by Orwell, the de Beauvoirs elevated vague standards about 'breeding' and 'good taste' to semi-religious importance, in order to stress that in spite of living on a proletarian income they could be distinguished from the proletariat by virtue of their education and manners.[2]

When Simone entered the Sorbonne, and began to acquire independence from her family in terms of her social contacts and the influences upon her, she inevitably began to see the terrible emptiness of the standards by which her parents, and in particular her mother, were trying to live. Their standards provided nothing, neither material rewards, nor social status, nor relevance of any kind to France of the late 1920s. Moreover, adherence to the values of this world could bring with it the kind of personal heartbreak that de Beauvoir observed in the case of her friend Elizabeth Mabille. This instance provided a second, highly emotionally charged reason why de Beauvoir came at such an early age to reject the values of her parents' world. Elizabeth Mabille, a schoolfriend of de Beauvoir's, came from a well-to-do Catholic family. For Elizabeth, it was a matter of some importance to fulfil the traditional expectations of her mother. Hence Elizabeth, an intellectually gifted girl, would spend hours occupied in trivial domestic work. But most important of all, she felt obliged by her mother's strict notions about relationships between the sexes to give up a man whom she deeply loved. The conflicts created by this situation were such that Elizabeth developed meningitis and subsequently died. For de Beauvoir, this tragedy demonstrated that values can be life-and-death matters, particularly when the values in question are associated with emotionally powerful figures, or conflict with rational understanding.

De Beauvoir's account of Elizabeth Mabille's death suggests that she saw it very much as a case of 'there but for fortune'. In de Beauvoir's case the fortune which saved her from the same fate was the poverty of her parents (there were few domestic or social tasks to undertake in their household and the penniless de Beauvoir girls did not have to be guarded from unscrupulous dowry hunters) and the degree of emotional detachment from her parents which she had achieved by her late adolescence. This element then contributes the third reason for de Beauvoir's disengagement from her background and her parents' world. No absolute rift occurred between de Beauvoir and her mother and her father, but throughout *Memoirs of a Dutiful Daughter* shifts take place in her views of her parents. This would be expected of all children as they gain maturity, but in de Beauvoir's case the estrangement from her parents is given a heightened importance because of the complexities of rejection and identification that can be discerned.

De Beauvoir's parents appear, in the first book of *Memoirs of a Dutiful Daughter*, as a happy and loving couple. Madame de Beauvoir was nine years junior to her husband, the daughter of a rich and devout bourgeois family. Simone's father was a lawyer, a man who departed every morning for the Law Courts 'carrying a briefcase stuffed with untouchable things called dossiers under his arm' (MDD, 6). Husband and wife, in the years of their early prosperity, had a close and amicable relationship, the husband delighting in his pretty and well-dressed wife, and the wife admiring her husband's greater worldliness and vivacity. But as the husband's fortunes declined, so apparently did the marriage – life with no money was no longer the gay and light-hearted affair that it had once been, and neither husband nor wife had the ability to adapt to straitened circumstances except by exaggerating the more negative aspects of their characters and personalities: the wife became more pious and unworldly, and the husband became more careless and increasingly absent. The father who had delighted in his daughter's academic success – when this had added to a rich life – came to be more distrustful of academic achievement when it appeared that her successes and her commitment to hard work would bring with them rewards that the affectations of careless brilliance could not achieve.

In de Beauvoir's father it is possible to see more than just a disappointed bourgeois: there is also a man who had impulses towards both creativity and order, an exaggerated inclination towards individuality coupled with a deep suspicion of the 'mass' or generalized categories of human beings, and a morality which is both fascinated and repelled by deviation. In de Beauvoir's second novel, *The Blood of Others*, one of the characters says of the middle class that 'they have a mania for not being like other people', and it would appear that her father shared this mania. Although, as a lawyer, he followed a most conventional profession, he had a real love for the theatre and would apparently have become a professional actor if his background had been such as to accommodate the idea of the theatre as a profession rather than an entertainment. Since he could not become a professional actor, it would appear that what Monsieur de Beauvoir did was to become something of an amateur actor, both in the sense that he took part in amateur theatricals and also – and more significantly – in that he adopted for himself a certain part to play in life. As his daughter was to write in *Memoirs of a Dutiful Daughter*:

'His name, certain family connections, childhood friends, and those he associated with as a young man convinced him that he belonged to the aristocracy, so he adopted their manner of living. He appreciated elegant gestures, charming compliments, social graces, style, frivolity, irony, all the free-and-easy self-assurance of the rich and the well-born. The more serious virtues esteemed by the bourgeoisie he found frankly boring. Thanks to a very good memory, he passed his examinations, but his student days were devoted mainly to pleasure: theatres, races, cafes and parties. He cared so little for the common run of success that once he had passed his qualifying examinations he didn't bother to present a thesis but registered himself in the Court of Appeal and took a post as secretary to a well established lawyer. He was contemptuous of successes which are obtained at the expense of hard work and effort: according to him, if you were 'born' to be someone, you automatically possessed all the essential qualities – wit, talent, charm and good breeding. The trouble was that in the ranks of that high society to which he laid claim for admittance, he found he was a nobody.'

(MDD, 33)

Here, then, was a man possessed of all the necessary qualifications to pass himself off as one of nature's aristocrats: except, of course, that after the First World War he became virtually penniless and barely able to support his family. Deeply imbued with all the values of the *ésprit boulevardier*, Monsieur de Beauvoir could not reconcile himself to the humdrum requirements of making a living and providing for his family. In this context Simone's academic achievements took on a double-edged meaning. As has been suggested earlier, Monsieur de Beauvoir admired intelligent women. De Beauvoir writes of his view that 'in order to shine . . . a woman should not only be beautiful and elegant but should also be well-read and a good conversationalist; so he was pleased by my early scholastic successes' (MDD, 176). But she continues:

'though my father liked intelligent and witty women, he had no time for blue stockings. When he announced: "My dears, you'll never marry: you'll have to work for your livings", there was bitterness in his voice. I believed he was being sorry for us; but in our hard-working futures he only saw his own failure; he was crying out against the injustice of a fate which condemned him to have daughters who could not keep up the social position he had given them.'

(MDD, 176)

For his daughters, and most particularly Simone, fate seemed to have offered not a harsh lot in life, but one that held out the chance of freedom and emancipation. From her father, de Beauvoir had been able to take a healthy scepticism and respect for intelligence; these essential elements had provided the basis from which she was to come to question the nature of the views which he held. From her mother, de Beauvoir seems to have acquired a certain respect for the tenacity with which women can maintain their values and beliefs in the face of male

hostility. Madame de Beauvoir's 'warmth of affection' is explicitly
stated in *A Very Easy Death*, and that book, a moving account of her
death, could hardly have been written by a daughter indifferent to her
mother. Indeed de Beauvoir is in many ways more explicit about her
mother in *A Very Easy Death* than in *Memoirs*. In the former, the intense
physical passion between her parents, its subsequent decline into
indifference, her father's petty philanderings, and her mother's furious,
yet passive, resignation to her fate are all stated very much more
clearly. So, too, is the part that Madame de Beauvoir took in fighting
for her daughters' interests. Thus, for example, Monsieur de Beauvoir:

> 'held it against my sister that she would not sacrifice her vocation
> as a painter in order to earn her bread and butter, and that she
> went on living at home: he would not give her a penny and he
> barely fed her. Maman stood up for her and used all her ingenuity
> to help her.'
>
> (VED, 36)

What emerges from the mixture of her parents' personalities is a
situation in which Simone and, to a lesser extent, her younger sister
were given conflicting views about the world, real kindness and concern in their childhood, and consistent interest, if not agreement, in
their adult lives. The family was in no sense in full accord; in *Memoirs* de
Beauvoir frequently refers to other families as 'well-integrated' and
that is certainly not an epithet that could be applied to her own. The
difference in attitude to religion between de Beauvoir's parents was just
one aspect, albeit the most serious, of the other discrepancies in values
between husband and wife. Two aspects of these discrepancies are
perhaps particularly significant in terms of Simone's future development. The first is that many of the disagreements between the de
Beauvoirs were never expressed, and the second the different symbolic
structures represented for de Beauvoir by her mother and her father: the
father representing, and lauding, intelligence, education, and independent action, the mother personifying emotional warmth and
unstated female strength – the traditional martyred wife who maintains her own values and her own integrity by the passive rejection of
the standards of the male world and by the elevation of spiritual values.
As de Beauvoir was to write of her parents: 'I grew accustomed to the
idea that my intellectual life – embodied by my father – and my spiritual
life – expressed by my mother – were radically heterogenous fields of
experience which had absolutely nothing in common' (MDD, 41). This
aspect of de Beauvoir's work and development will be discussed later:
here it is sufficient to note that in the context of her parents' marriage

she saw manifested vividly that disjunction between men and culture on the one hand, and women and nature on the other, which has been identified by feminism as a constant feature of many cultures.

The other aspect of the de Beauvoirs' marriage observed by their daughter, and one which also constitutes a commonly noticed feature of many social relationships (not least those between the sexes), was the fabric of convenient lies, half-truths, and strategic evasions. In the case of the de Beauvoirs' marriage all of these means of turning away from the harsh truth were often employed. De Beauvoir writes that:

> 'More than once, between the age of fifteen and twenty, I saw him (my father) coming home at eight in the morning, smelling of drink, and telling confused tales of bridge or poker. Maman made no scenes: perhaps she believed him, so trained was she at running away from awkward truths. But she could not happily adapt herself to his indifference. Her case alone would be enough to convince me that bourgeois marriage is an unnatural institution. The wedding ring on her finger had authorised her to become acquainted with pleasure; her senses had grown demanding; at thirty-five, in the prime of her life, she was no longer allowed to satisfy them.'

(VED, 32)

Hence in de Beauvoir's account of her mother's life, both in *A Very Easy Death* and *Memoirs of a Dutiful Daughter*, a vein of deep, irritated affection can be detected, an affection that was not properly appreciated until the death of the mother. De Beauvoir writes of her mother that she was 'passionate and headstrong', characteristics that can also be detected in herself and which are likely to inspire intense emotions in others. Yet for all the positive feelings that Madame de Beauvoir could inspire in her daughter, she could at least in equal part create feelings of rage and resentment. In de Beauvoir's early years – until the time of her economic emancipation from her parents – this took the form of immense irritation that she could be controlled by a woman whose views she regarded, certainly after the age of 14, as ridiculous. In later years, when de Beauvoir came to reflect on the reasons for her mother's behaviour – rather than simply putting her energies into escaping from the same fate – she can hardly have felt anything except furious rage at the way in which people, and particularly women, refuse to recognize the reality of their situation and, rather than confront issues and patterns of behaviour with which they disagree, employ circuitous means to secure their own interests. De Beauvoir's mother represents an excellent example of much of traditional female behaviour that contemporary feminism has so actively rejected: the passive suffering, the suppressed rage, and the implicit refusal to reject male control and male identification are all features of women's accommodation to patriarchal oppression which has been the subject of attack by the feminist movement. As an adolescent girl in France in the 1920s, de Beauvoir can scarcely have been aware of the generality of women's furious, quiet resentment at their fate which has been demonstrated and articulated by contemporary feminism. Many other adolescent girls, particularly from bourgeois or petit-bourgeois families, might have reasoned that the cause of their mother's unhappiness was an unlucky choice of husband (the 'wrong man' theory of conjugal misery), and been primarily concerned in their own lives to make a better choice. What caused de Beauvoir to follow another path, to assert an independent identity and establish a life that did not depend on marriage and economic and social dependence on a man cannot be explained by a single factor. Among the factors which may have directed de Beauvoir towards autonomy, intellectual life, and independence, three features of her emotional and social background were perhaps crucial. In emotional terms it is apparent that de Beauvoir's father represented a pattern of personal autonomy denied to her mother: men could apparently control their destinies in a way which women could not. The limitations of this view – of assuming that the male world identified with rationality and personal independence constitutes freedom – were to manifest themselves both in de Beauvoir's personal life and in her work. But to an adolescent girl, observing the relative positions of her mother and her father, and at the same time imbued with an almost spiritual respect for the truth, the world of men can hardly have seemed anything except attractive.

Yet motivation and an emotional predisposition towards education and its rewards might have come to nothing if other structural features of de Beauvoir's social background had been absent. First, there was the crucial fact that de Beauvoir had to provide for herself. Since she came from a bourgeois family, with a father who despite his own lackadaisical energies could appreciate excellence and originality in others, it is not surprising that de Beauvoir did not think simply in terms of earning her living – as a girl from a proletarian family would have done – but thought instead in terms of a career, of a life of committed work and exceptional achievement. Thus we can detect in the experiences of her early life, and in the values of her parents, the impetus towards achievement and self-realization. Hence, though doing something exceptional in training to be a teacher of philosophy, she was not challenging the essential values of her class by her engagement in academic competition. The similarity here between de Beauvoir's career and that of other feminists is important: de Beauvoir, and other bourgeois women in other societies, worked hard to enter professions but in doing so they did not defy the central bourgeois value of individual competition against others for material rewards and social status.

The second feature of de Beauvoir's background which made it possible for her to diverge from the normal path of bourgeois womanhood was the simple, but absolutely crucial, fact of her residence in Paris where élite educational institutions were accessible. In a society like that of France which is highly centralized, the opportunities available to de Beauvoir in Paris would simply not have existed in the provinces. The Sorbonne, the great majority of the *grandes écoles*, and the whole cultural life of the society were, and are, located in Paris. Throughout de Beauvoir's life she quite unconsciously reflects the unquestioned assumption of the French intellectual élite that all cultural and artistic life takes place in Paris. To Anglo-Saxon and North American audiences this emphasis on one city may seem bizarre, but de Beauvoir, like her educated contemporaries, viewed the world outside Paris as some kind of Stygian wilderness, occasionally important for the possibilities it offered for recuperation in the countryside but otherwise synonymous with narrow-mindedness, superstition, and boredom. In the years which de Beauvoir spent outside Paris (the period 1931–38) she consistently passed as much as possible of her leisure in Paris, and her return to residence in Paris she recalls with all the fervour of one returning from exile.

Two factors favouring possible emancipation through education thus existed for de Beauvoir: she had access to the means of education, and her background encouraged achievement and competition. A third factor which must be considered is that the alternatives offered to de Beauvoir did not attract her. She was scarcely an attractive match for ambitious young men of her own class: having no dowry and a reputation for social awkwardness and unconventionality, she lacked the basic requirements of a good bourgeois wife. But even if she had been chosen, the possibility of marriage clearly did not attract her. The one serious relationship of her adolescent years – with a cousin named Jacques – was beset with the kind of equivocation, calculation, and underlying concern for social niceties that de Beauvoir had already rejected, and had identified as in large part the cause of the fundamental dishonesty of her parents' marriage. It is clear that Jacques and de Beauvoir were strongly attracted to one another, yet Jacques was unable to transcend the limits of the expectations of his family, and de Beauvoir herself was not yet at the point in her life where she could exercise the degree of personal choice which she was to display in the establishment of her relationship with Sartre.

Just as Book Two of *Memoirs of a Dutiful Daughter* begins when the de Beauvoirs move house, so Books Three and Four begin with major changes in de Beauvoir's life. Book Three is marked by her transfer from the Cours Désir to the Institut Sainte-Marie, Book Four begins as de Beauvoir enters the final stage of her studies for the *agrégation* (the competitive examination for teachers in secondary and higher education). But none of these changes has anything like as much importance in de Beauvoir's eyes as the major events that occur between *Memoirs of a Dutiful Daughter* and *The Prime of Life*: the beginning of her relationship with Sartre and the death of Elizabeth Mabille. The latter event was a source of great unhappiness to de Beauvoir; equally it was something of a vindication since de Beauvoir, in rejecting the values and habits of her world, clearly feels that she – unlike Elizabeth – escaped with her life. Moreover, the death of Elizabeth occurred at a time when de Beauvoir was cutting a number of her previous ties; the friends of her early days at the Sorbonne were being slowly discarded in favour of Sartre and the circle around him. In a sense, it is difficult not to feel that if Elizabeth had not died, de Beauvoir would have anyway abandoned all ties with her: in the world which she was entering there was less and less place for those bound by the moral and religious systems that she had come to despise.

The latter pages of *Memoirs of a Dutiful Daughter* document the death of Elizabeth, and suggest the beginnings of de Beauvoir's friendship with Sartre. 'From now on I'm going to take you under my wing', said Sartre to the young de Beauvoir and it proved to be the beginning of a life-long relationship – even if it very rapidly becomes clear that Sartre's protective wing was not large enough to encompass de Beauvoir. Their partnership is a well-documented and fascinating instance of a relationship between a man and a woman, although today its structural unorthodoxy might appear simply slightly unconventional, while other aspects of the relationship between Sartre and de Beauvoir might be interpreted as an only too familiar instance of the inequalities between the sexes. Again, contemporary feminism must make us examine more critically the assumption that de Beauvoir and Sartre established a relationship different in its essential emotional and sexual assumptions from those of the conventional world: merely in terms of the services which they provided for each other, it is apparent that on many occasions de

Beauvoir fulfilled the traditional female role of nurturing and assuming domestic responsibilities. During the Second World War it was de Beauvoir who scoured Paris for food, and cooked, and during the last ten years of Sartre's life – when he was terribly enfeebled and often ill – it was de Beauvoir who cared for him and tried to mitigate his suffering. The only documented domestic task which Sartre undertook was to carry a plate of the *plat du jour* to de Beauvoir when she was ill.

But judgements and speculations on their relationship in 1928 were not about the power relations between the sexes, or the division of domestic labour; they were about the more mundane and common-place matters of the loss of de Beauvoir's 'honour' and her apparently inevitable future as a lost woman. Part One, chapter one of *The Prime of Life* opens with de Beauvoir preparing her new, independent home in Paris and waiting for the return of Sartre to Paris after the summer holidays. There is more than an element of the young bride awaiting the arrival of her new husband in these first three pages: the new furniture is brought, the walls papered, and new clothes purchased. Then, the ground prepared, the decisive event occurs. Or, as de Beauvoir puts it, 'My new life really began when Sartre returned to Paris in mid-October.'

The young couple then threw themselves into an orgy of discussion and exploration, and the first chapter of *The Prime of Life* radiates de Beauvoir's sheer delight and excitement at having found a man who could appeal to so many of her senses. Like many couples, the pair rapidly developed their own private jokes and points of reference: they occasionally assumed false names (Mr and Mrs Morgan Hattick and Monsieur and Madame M. Organatique) which reflect the nature of their relationship as they conceived it at the time. With no direct reference to the matter de Beauvoir and Sartre became lovers, de Beauvoir having already prepared the justification for this in *Memoirs of a Dutiful Daughter* in her attack on the bourgeois double standard of sexual morality. Inevitably, de Beauvoir's parents were less than delighted with the course that their daughter's life was taking. However, such had been the alienation between parents and daughter that occurred during her adolescence that this last example of her distance seems to have been accepted with a resigned shrug. De Beauvoir's father clearly had no misunderstanding about his daughter's relationship with Sartre ('She's on her Paris honeymoon', de Beauvoir remembers him saying) but her mother seemed less willing to accept her daughter's new life. Nevertheless, by this time de Beauvoir was so far from the sphere of their influence that neither shock nor disgusted innuendo could make any difference.

But gradually the tone of *The Prime of Life* changes: the heady rapture of the first months of the relationship shifts into a far more sober consideration, on both sides, of what kind of future the relationship would have. It is now that some of the differences in expectations between Sartre and de Beauvoir, general differences that are common to many men and women, become marked. On the fundamental principles of the relationship there appeared to be no real disagreement; neither wished to marry or have children. The pair did consider marriage, at a point where it would have been more convenient for their professional life, but it was a possibility that they both resisted. There was enough of the conventional petit-bourgeois girl left in de Beauvoir for her to say, of her decision not to marry Sartre, that 'Marriage doubles one's domestic responsibilities, and, indeed all one's social chores' (PL, 77). Marriage is not understood here as a private matter between two adults: what is being invoked is a social relationship, and one that carries with it certain inescapable commitments and responsibilities. The possibility of living in a marriage in such a way as to refuse these obligations was clearly not entertained by either party. Neither did the establishment of a common home seem to appeal to de Beauvoir and Sartre; during all their lives they were never to live in the same domestic space, although they generally lived in close physical proximity to each other.

With marriage and the establishment of a joint household rejected, largely because of the conventional expectations associated with them, the only other factor that might have bound Sartre and de Beauvoir together in something approaching domestic normality was the desire for children. This, de Beauvoir writes, was something that 'we did not possess'. In a paragraph, neatly compartmentalized as the sole discussion in her entire work about her views on her own possible career as a mother, she relates that she has no 'prejudice against motherhood as such' but that her happiness with Sartre was too complete 'for any new element to attract me'. She writes:

> '(Sartre) was sufficient both for himself and for me. I too was self sufficient: I never once dreamed of rediscovering myself in the child I might bear. In any case, I felt such absence of affinity with my own parents that any sons or daughters I might have I regarded in advance as strangers; from them I expected either indifference or hostility – so great had been my own aversion to family life.'
>
> (PL, 77–8)

So children are written out of de Beauvoir's – and Sartre's – life. The new self-consciousness about motherhood (and indeed fatherhood) created in the past twenty years should not make us expect that those individuals who write their memoirs should write a great deal about this aspect of adult life; but even so it is perhaps strange that de Beauvoir says so little about this subject.

In particular, two aspects of de Beauvoir's remarks about children are curious and, in the context of the life of a woman identified as a feminist, important. First, it is remarkable that de Beauvoir so completely isolates the question of bearing children from the discussion of heterosexuality. She does not write a great deal about the more intimate aspects of her relationship with Sartre, but the three or four sentences she gives to the description of their lives as lovers suggest a passionate warmth. Moreover, as she is to discuss in the early pages of *The Prime of Life*, de Beauvoir is a woman who finds pleasure in heterosexuality: the absence of Sartre in those early days did not just bring nostalgia for his cerebral qualities, and in a later volume of her memoirs de Beauvoir is again to reveal (and again express succinctly) that she was physically delighted by the beginning of a new love affair and had not accepted easily a chaste existence. Just as de Beauvoir's mother had amazed her daughter at the transformation which sexuality could produce in her, so in her turn her daughter is amazed at the strength of her own desires. All the more curious then, that she does not reflect a little more on the construction of those desires, or even consider the way in which heterosexual pleasure may, or may not, be related to the desire for children. Further, it is remarkable that a woman who could delight so strongly in sensual pleasure (and recall the physical delights of her own childhood so vividly) was not a little more attracted to the possibility of recreating those days for herself.

Yet the birth of children, as Hegel once said (and as de Beauvoir reiterates in *The Second Sex*), is often the death of parents. Perhaps in de Beauvoir's disinclination to have children there lay an unacknowledged realization that this development was incompatible with the relationship with Sartre: the very relationship that might have created the desire for maternity could not survive the consummation of that desire – unlike the relationship with Jacques, whose more conventional qualities made motherhood a more attractive, and feasible, possibility. In her assessment of Sartre's competence as a father, de Beauvoir's projections clearly rapidly foundered on the realization that his life was not, in any sense, about social reproduction. Equally, we might conjecture that those needs in women for intimacy and creativity, which can be fulfilled by motherhood rather than by relations with men, were met, in the case of de Beauvoir, by her relationship with Sartre: as she says, 'my happiness was complete'. Motherhood, feminist literature of recent years has demonstrated, alters in radical ways the relationship of husband and wife, and of women to men. Given that society assigns to women the large part of responsibility for the everyday care of children, women with children are involved in very different emotions, needs, and activities from those of men. In *Memoirs of a Dutiful Daughter* de Beauvoir wrote that 'It is tolerably well known that in men habit kills desire'; in *The Second Sex* she was to write that: 'It is significant that woman . . . requires help in performing the function assigned to her by nature. . . . At just the time when woman attains the realisation of her feminine destiny, she is still dependent' (SS, 476).

In these two remarks we can, perhaps, perceive something more of de Beauvoir's own views on motherhood and heterosexuality than she expresses openly: a perception that marriages, and heterosexual relationships in general, can seldom be maintained by physical attraction, and that motherhood is a state which much reduces women's autonomy and the attention which they can devote to relationships with adults. De Beauvoir had seen for herself, in her parents' marriage, the slow decline of a relationship founded in large part on mutual physical attraction. She was also obviously perceptive enough to appreciate that with Sartre a conventional marriage, and parenthood, might well become a burden to them both.

It was thus of great importance to de Beauvoir, although it would appear much less so to Sartre, to identify their relationship in terms other than those of the conventional world, but it was essentially Sartre who explained to de Beauvoir what the nature of their relationship would be. First, Sartre made it plain that he 'was not inclined to be monogamous by nature: he took pleasure in the company of women, finding them less comic than men. He had no intention, at twenty three, of renouncing their tempting variety' (PL, 22). So Sartre did not attempt to conceal from de Beauvoir that at least for him their relationship was not going to be one of constant sexual fidelity. Perhaps in order to temper this revelation, Sartre explained that their relationship would have other contours than those of the strictest monogamy:

'He explained the matter to me in his favourite terminology. "What we have", he said, "is an essential love; but it is a good idea for us also to experience contingent love affairs." We were two of a kind, and our relationship would endure as long as we did.'

(PL, 22)

To de Beauvoir this identification with Sartre, and a certain set of shared values, are clearly of the utmost importance. She was to write that in her relationship with Sartre the central fact has to be recognized: 'the identical sign on both our brows' (PL, 25). Part of that sign, and part of the pact between de Beauvoir and Sartre, was the commitment which Sartre gave de Beauvoir, and which he made a second feature of the relationship: that they would tell each other everything.

These two suggestions, indeed conditions, namely complete honesty and no commitment to sexual fidelity, on which Sartre established his relationship with de Beauvoir, gave rise to numerous problems in subsequent years.[3] De Beauvoir had observed in her parents' marriage the concealed realities, the lies, and the evasions which had been essential to the continuation of the marriage: in her relationship with Sartre she was to enter an even more complicated world than that of orthodox petit-bourgeois deceit and adultery – a world of apparent honesty in which in some crucial senses all was known and nothing was told. The complications of the pact which de Beauvoir and Sartre made arose therefore, not out of humdrum deceits, the 'ordinary' lies of many marriages and many extramarital affairs, but out of a commitment in which two people had bound themselves to be truthful but then found that the freedoms which they had assured each other made it impossible, or at least very difficult, for them to be absolutely honest without shattering a much valued relationship. For feminists and indeed any student of male/female relationships, the nature of this relationship raises fundamental questions about the ways in which men and women can live together in relationships of honesty and trust, without imposing on either party bonds of oppressive or distorting constraint. The price of heterosexual fidelity, the cost to both men and women of infidelity, and the agonies of passion, jealousy, emotional loss, and sexual exclusivity are all raised by Sartre and de Beauvoir both in the course of their relationship with each other, and in their fictional discussions of these issues.

In the course of their joint lives, both Sartre and de Beauvoir were to have relationships with others that were both significant and, in three cases, potentially threatening to the stability of their understanding: the relationship of Sartre and Olga, of Sartre and 'M', and of de Beauvoir and Nelson Algren. There were other affairs, particularly on Sartre's side, but they were essentially of a fleeting kind. In the case of the more serious relationships which he had with women other than de Beauvoir, Sartre seems to have maintained at least a partial honesty: in the case of others he quite candidly admitted that he lied. Writing of

Olivier Todd's account of his friendship with Sartre, Douglas Johnson notes that:

> 'Although Simone de Beauvoir has written about the pact which she and Sartre had made together, whereby the one would never lie to the other, Todd recounts that once, when he asked Sartre how he managed to navigate amongst his many affairs with women, his "amours contingentes", the reply was that he lied to them. It was, Sartre explained, simpler and more honest. "You lie to them all?" queried Todd. "To them all", replied Sartre with a smile. "*Même au Castor?*" "*Surtout au Castor.*"'[4]

So Sartre's interpretation of the absolute honesty that he had pledged to de Beauvoir was not one that adherents of the view that truth is only and always a form of words would find that he had complied with. Sartre clearly knew that, in the literal sense, he was lying, yet in another sense his words quoted above suggest that to him questions about truth and dishonesty involved more than verbal answers to particular questions. What is apparently being invoked here is an understanding of honesty (and deceit) in terms of actions and intent. This hypothesis can be illustrated by Sartre's reply to the question put to him by de Beauvoir at a time when his relationship with 'M' was at its most passionate. Unable to fight her jealousy, and wracked by fears that the relationship between herself and Sartre is about to end, de Beauvoir asked Sartre who meant the most to him. Sartre's reply was that 'M' means a great deal to him, but he is with de Beauvoir (FC, 69). Whatever other half-truths or lies about the relationship Sartre has told, he is perhaps suggesting that his intention, an intention from which he apparently never wavered, was to maintain the relationship with de Beauvoir. If he had answered de Beauvoir with absolute honesty, then perhaps their relationship would have been seriously endangered, and both parties would have been forced into making the kinds of choices and decisions which could only have led to the destruction of their friendship: Sartre would have been exposed as a fairly consistent liar (at least in the context of his sexual life), and de Beauvoir would have shown herself as someone who despite her earlier commitment to allow Sartre his freedom was not in fact prepared to do so. Sartre's deceit about his affairs might, then, be balanced by a kind of dishonesty on de Beauvoir's part: though she was deeply hurt and upset by Sartre's infidelities, she would allow herself to be deceived rather than face the rupture of a relationship which her autobiography asserts was of fundamental importance to her.

The many situations in which Sartre had occasion to lie to de Beauvoir do not – since this is not a history of Sartre's romantic life – concern us here. What is important about the relationship between Sartre and de Beauvoir in the context of an examination of de Beauvoir's work and its relationship to feminism is whether or not the relationship was structured and determined by generally observed patterns in the relations of men and women, and whether the relationship did give to both parties equal rewards and satisfactions, albeit of different kinds. De Beauvoir has been the more forthcoming of the two on the history of their friendship, while Sartre maintained a more or less complete silence, expressing his views on heterosexuality and his relations with women largely in the context of interviews conducted by de Beauvoir herself. One feature of these interviews and of de Beauvoir's writings on her personal life is immediately striking: Sartre discusses women as a general category when interviewed by de Beauvoir, de Beauvoir writes of particular men (and most specifically of course Sartre) in her autobiography. Men as a category appear as little in her work as specific women appear in Sartre's. From this it could be inferred that for Sartre, relations with women were always (except in the case of de Beauvoir) associated with generalized needs: Sartre seldom devotes a great deal of attention to the detailed workings of the psyche of the women with whom he is involved, whereas de Beauvoir explores at some length the background, tastes, and talents of Sartre and the two other men (Nelson Algren and Claude Lanzmann) with whom she had significant relationships.

In their different discussions and emphases of their emotional and sexual relationships, de Beauvoir and Sartre illustrate a pattern which has often been noted in the west: that men see women, other than those blessed with the title of wife and mother, as generalized others, and make the kind of distinctions – between goddesses and whores, and significant and insignificant others – that are only possible for the sex which has at its command the control of the ideology of sexuality. Women, on the other hand, who cannot view men as a generalized source of sexual satisfaction, since the cost of implementing this view carries with it social stigmatization, are encouraged to develop an understanding of the sexual and emotional world in which only one man can reveal to them the secrets of both the universe and the orgasm. De Beauvoir, by her own admission in *The Prime of Life*, had realized that she had a nature which delighted in the physical expression of sexuality. Yet at the same time as she realized this, she also acknowledged that her body had the potential of becoming a 'poisoned shirt'.

She writes:

> 'In the feverish caresses and love-making that bound me to the
> man of my choice I could discern the movements of my heart, my
> freedom as an individual. But that mood of solitary, languorous
> excitement cried out for anyone, regardless.'

(PL, 63)

Sartre had revealed to de Beauvoir her potential for sexual pleasure
and enjoyment, but Sartre was not always there to satisfy those needs,
nor, it is clear, was he prepared to confine his sexual activities to the
relationship with de Beauvoir. Like all women who have realized their
capacity for sexual enjoyment, and are nevertheless unwilling to
embark on a career of sexual promiscuity, de Beauvoir had come to see
that the possibilities of sexual pleasure are equalled, given the way that
sexual and emotional values are constructed, only by their difficulties.
Nor is de Beauvoir alone in this realization. The history of western
literature abounds with instances of women crying out, like Jane Eyre,
for the 'busy world, towns, regions full of life I had heard of but never
seen – that then I desired more of practical experience than I
possessed',[5] or like Sylvia Plath, openly envying men the freedoms they
are allowed:

> 'I am jealous of men – a dangerous and subtle envy which can
> corrode, I imagine, any relationship. It is an envy born of the
> desire to be active and doing, not passive and listening. I envy the
> man his physical freedom to lead a double life – his career, and his
> sexual and family life.'

(Plath 1982:35)

So when Sartre sat and outlined his plans for his life to de Beauvoir –
relationships with other women and the exploration of the numerous
social possibilities of the world – it is difficult not to look for the same
outline of life from de Beauvoir. Equally, it is inconceivable that it
could be there: women have never had the freedom to roam the world
and explore its public places. In France (indeed anywhere in Europe)
in the 1920s and 1930s, bourgeois, respectable women did not walk the
streets from morning till night, travel alone, live alone, or enter into
sexual relationships with men to whom they were not married. The
anonymity of Paris must have allowed de Beauvoir a good deal of
freedom which would not have been hers in the provinces; even so,
constraints on her behaviour (and she points this out when noting how
her habits and friendships elicited gossip when she was teaching in
Rouen) did exist, and throughout her life she had to endure barbed

remarks from conventional society about her way of life and her
relationship with Sartre.

Among the many pressures on the relationship was de Beauvoir's
own fear of becoming dependent on Sartre. Early in their relationship
she wrote that: 'I reflected that to adapt one's outlook to another
person's salvation is the surest and quickest way of losing him' (PL,
62). Independence, autonomy, and a literary career were therefore
attractive to de Beauvoir both in themselves and terms of the
possibilities that they offered for maintaining the relationship with
Sartre. Far from being threatened by a woman's independence, Sartre
was worried by dependence and chided de Beauvoir: '"You used to be
full of little ideas, Beaver," he said, in an astonished voice. He also told
me to watch out that I didn't become a female introvert' (PL, 61).
Nevertheless, the pressures on de Beauvoir – both from herself and
from Sartre – to make herself more than just a woman of Sartre's, while
considerable, cannot account for all her motivation. It is apparent that
she wished to write, and live her own life in her own way, long before
she met Sartre. But she was also aware of the trap of personal
happiness: of finding a partner who matched her dreams and wrapping
herself in a world of private enjoyments. In later chapters, de
Beauvoir's constant reiteration of the theme of the woman who gives up
all for the love of a particular man will be discussed. Here it is sufficient
to say that de Beauvoir was saved from absorption in personal
happiness and over-dependence on a male other both by her own
determination and by the incident of the trio. Thus in order to assert her
independence she took a job in Marseilles, miles from Paris and Sartre.
As she says:

> 'In the whole of my life I have experienced no special moment
> that I can label "decisive"; but certain occasions have become so
> charged with significance in retrospect that they stand out from
> my past as clearly as if they had been truly great events. Looking
> back, I feel that my arrival in Marseilles marked a completely new
> turn to my career.'
>
> (PL, 88)

The year which de Beauvoir spent in Marseilles was not marked by
incidents of great personal significance; rather, the importance of the
year was that it was perceived by de Beauvoir as a successful lesson in
self-reliance: 'I was emerging triumphant from the trials to which I had
been subjected: separation and loneliness had not destroyed my peace
of mind. I knew that I could now rely on myself (PL, 112–13). But this
confident sense of self-hood was soon to be tested by an incident of far

greater significance than temporary physical separation from Sartre. The incident was that of the trio; the prospect that it raised was that of the loss of Sartre's affections and his love for another woman.

The episode of the trio, outlined in full in fact in *The Prime of Life* and in fiction in *She Came to Stay*, both caused de Beauvoir acute mental pain and made her physically ill. Self-reliance, it became clear, was not sufficient armour against the possibility of emotional loss. The third party, the 'other', in the trio was named Olga, a student at the *lycée* in Rouen where de Beauvoir was teaching. For a variety of reasons, de Beauvoir and Sartre decided to adopt Olga and help her to escape from provincial life. Rapidly, the relationship turned sour, and the three became involved in a circle of emotional competition, exclusiveness, and jealousy – a circle which moved more and more towards the establishment of a new couple of Sartre and Olga. De Beauvoir was trapped by her own initial commitment to the relationship and by her expressed avowal that she would never attempt to limit Sartre's freedom. What results is a tangle of conflicting emotions, broken eventually by Olga's departure from the trio (she forms a relationship with another student) and de Beauvoir's illness.

Sartre's views on the trio, and indeed on his emotional life with de Beauvoir, must remain a matter of conjecture. What has been documented is that Sartre explicitly separated de Beauvoir from other women, and that her powerful rational qualities may well have disguised, at least to him, her emotional torments and jealousies. From the interviews which de Beauvoir conducted with Sartre in the 1970s (ES) a picture of Sartre's sexual history emerges which conforms as much to a traditional masculine pattern as aspects of de Beauvoir's do to that traditionally expected of women. Sartre's initial sexual encounters were not with women with whom he formed lasting relationships; they were the typical sexual encounters of the young male bourgeois, sowing his wild oats with girls like the daughter of the concierge, girls who – in Sartre's words – '*couchait facilement*' (ES, 37). So while for de Beauvoir sexual initiation was reserved for 'the man of my choice' who revealed to her 'my freedom as an individual' (PL, 63), Sartre was far less interested in the particular qualities of an individual woman, and manifestly did not expect sexual activity to be confined to one specific person. By his own admission, Sartre was quite happy if women were pretty, and appealing, and interested in him. As de Beauvoir points out, the implication of this is that any woman who decided to enter a relationship with Sartre could do so. 'My God', said Sartre when confronted with this revelation and the implicit suggestion that he had an apparently insatiable desire and ability to please women (ES, 378). The appeal of women, he continued, was generally not highly individuated (in the sense of a particular woman having particular qualities) but general – the promise and allure of sentimentality and sensibility. Women offered, therefore, not the realization of structured relationships but the development of feelings and possibilities assumed to have little place in the 'real' world – a world which both Sartre and de Beauvoir agreed was that of political and intellectual life.

In the course of his conversations with de Beauvoir on sexual relations Sartre made a distinction which provides a fascinating insight into the way in which they both saw human beings. In discussing his views on women Sartre stated that what made women fascinating to him was the way in which they can combine intelligence and '*la sensibilité*' – an instinct and capacity for feeling which men apparently lack. Thus while men tend to subordinate their emotional life to reason and rationality, women feel under no such pressure and are able to exhibit a fuller humanity and more diverse set of responses than men. Sartre explicitly stated that he did not regard women as any less intelligent than men, but for various reasons their intelligence is less developed – certainly not organized in those often inhibiting and over-scholastic ways which can be features of a traditional 'male' education. Describing his many affairs and close friendships with women, Sartre stressed again their '*sensibilite*' but also added that women, by virtue of their marginality, are often a good deal more interesting than men: creatures who are less integrated into the central values of the society and thus much better able to maintain a critical distance from the social world. Yet in spite of this eulogy of women, Sartre then remarked that it was only with de Beauvoir, of all his women friends, that he had been able to live in the 'real' world. With other women, Sartre described himself as having lived in '*une histoire*' (ES, 387), returning to de Beauvoir for an understanding of reality. Only de Beauvoir, Sartre stated, allowed him to live with a woman in his world of rational thought, literature, and politics. For the rest, the women – albeit loved and valued – represented the realization of almost masturbatory fantasies about the generalized female.

But while men can indulge – either through explicit sexual encounters, or pornography, or sexual fantasy – in the elaboration of their feelings and needs about women, western society does not allow women the same freedom. Thus while Sartre could explore, either in real or abstract terms, his sexual needs and desires, de Beauvoir was constrained by social mores from following a similar path. Despite the freedoms that de Beauvoir had won for herself – her economic emancipation and her social independence – her existence in the social world and her relationship with Sartre and with others was beset with the same constraints that affect all women. The moral structure of the west does not allow men and women the same freedoms, and in the relationship between Sartre and de Beauvoir it was de Beauvoir who was the deviant partner: a woman who departed from social expectations and conventions. The rewards of the relationship with Sartre are expressed frequently by de Beauvoir, but so too are the costs, and above all the terrible jealousy when Sartre embarked on significant relationships with others. De Beauvoir, like Sartre, seems to have something of a bourgeois hierarchy of sexual encounters: some women were fleeting sexual partners (like the women who were her father's occasional lovers) while a few others were more significant – and typically, those who could come closest to de Beauvoir herself in exhibiting certain rational qualities. When any of these women appeared to be intruding on the compact between herself and Sartre, de Beauvoir was subject to intense feelings of misery and loneliness.[6]

In the long history of the relationship between Sartre and de Beauvoir, it is impossible not to see the inequalities of personal suffering that derive less from the specific characteristics of individuals than from more generalized patterns of sexual relations.[7] Sartre, by his own admission, frequently lied to de Beauvoir, and in doing so followed the quite traditional path of anyone involved in an adulterous relationship. De Beauvoir, as far as we know, never lied to Sartre, but inevitably the possibility arises that she did not have to: that Sartre saw her engagement with others as neither threatening nor disturbing. We cannot, therefore, accuse Sartre of territoriality in his attitude to de Beauvoir: he was quite prepared to meet Nelson Algren in the most friendly and welcoming manner, and to continue his close friendship with Lanzmann, despite the involvement of both of them with de Beauvoir. The woman's involvement with other men did not arouse the same passions as the man's involvement with other women: in this distinction it is not, perhaps, too far-fetched to see at work the evaluation that both men and women place on both themselves and on their relationships with others. Moreover, it suggests that frequently observed situation in which women compete for men – not for their sexual favours (which would be the object of men's competition for women) but for something more intangible: an identification and an exclusivity with a particular man. De Beauvoir's advantage in her relationship with Sartre was always that sexual (and social) inequality made it virtually impossible for other women to acquire her rational skills, and demonstrate her rational competence. The weakness of de Beauvoir's position, or at any rate the aspect of the relationship with Sartre that was to bring her unhappiness, was that she could not admit her jealousies or her need for exclusivity without apparently abandoning her rationality. Thus de Beauvoir was frequently to devalue sexuality and sexual experience, and overemphasize rationality. In denying the importance of sexuality she could negate the importance of Sartre's affairs with other women, while in stressing the importance of the concerns of the 'real' world she in fact stressed the centrality of her own position in Sartre's life. The trap, or at any rate the constraint into which de Beauvoir was forced, was not the commonplace fate of women who are denied the opportunity to exercise their rational capacities, but that any departure from intellectual life or from the detachment which she had acquired would have made her come perilously close to inclusion in the general category of women: the creatures for whom Sartre reserved his emotional, but not his intellectual and rational life. This is not to say that de Beauvoir should have abandoned her intellectual pursuits for some romantic pursuit of feeling but that she was constrained by the way in which rationality and emotional life are perceived and dichotomized in western patriarchal culture into an occasional overemphasis on the rational aspects and qualities of human existence. In this constraint (the costs of which should not be exaggerated, since de Beauvoir clearly gained an enormous amount from her intellectual life) can be seen that dichotomy in western culture between men, who represent the intellect and culture in a general sense, and women – the creatures of nature and feeling.

The perception by de Beauvoir that with Sartre she would have to stress certain aspects of her personality and capabilities rather than others seems to have been made at an early stage in their relationship: she notes that she was aware that she had to avoid turning into a mere helpmeet of Sartre's, and *The Prime of Life* is essentially an account of her long road to independence. The novels and essays for which she was to acquire lasting fame did not emerge rapidly, and although she graduated from the Sorbonne at the age of 21, it was not until the age of 35 that her first novel was published. A long apprenticeship was to follow the initial commitment to write, and the determination to assert an identity independent of Sartre that had been forged in her early twenties. Even that determination, and a considerable intellectual competence, might never have been forged into the skills that were needed to write *The Mandarins* and *The Second Sex*, had not secure and total happiness disappeared. In a description of herself just before the outbreak of the Second World War de Beauvoir wrote:

'Literature appears when something in life goes slightly adrift. In order to write . . . the first essential condition is that *reality should no longer be taken for granted*; only then can one both perceive it, and make others do so. When I struggled free of the boredom and slavery of my childhood years, I was overwhelmed, stunned, blinded with sheer happiness. How could I ever have found in this blissful condition the urge to escape from it? My schemes of work remained futile dreams until the day came when that happiness was threatened, and I discovered a certain kind of solitude in anxiety. The unfortunate episode of the trio did much more than supply me with a subject for a novel; it enabled me to deal with it.'

(PL, 365)

So the threat of the loss of the relationship with Sartre is perceived by de Beauvoir herself as crucial in her development as a writer. She does not explore the reasons for this – other than implicitly suggesting that too much security does not develop a critical sense – and her readers can only conjecture that what forced de Beauvoir into true independence and autonomy (in the sense of the development of a capacity to objectify her relationships with others) was the loss of the special, exclusive bond that she had previously felt between Sartre and herself. When this bond was broken so too was de Beauvoir's illusion that she could establish her identity through another.[8]

Yet Sartre's infidelity cannot be identified as the single cause of de Beauvoir's emergence as a major literary figure. The roots of de Beauvoir's happiness – and unhappiness – lay in the structure of sexual relationships, relationships which denied, and deny, to both sexes the development of their varied human capacities. But to women, very much more than men, falls the cost of being forced to deny or limit their capacities for rational thought. That de Beauvoir did not accept this deforming ideology is a tribute to her will and talent, as was her ability to externalize the problems of the trio. De Beauvoir did not fall into that commonplace depression which women can feel when faced with the possible loss of the male other who confirms their identity and place in the world.[9] On the contrary, she sought to understand the issues raised by Sartre's involvement with Olga, and her own reactions to the situation. The work that emerged from that fractured reality is the subject of the following chapters, though all of it will be seen in the light of the constant tension in both the social world and de Beauvoir's personal world between the needs and desires of men and women.

2
_____Organizing principles_____

Simone de Beauvoir's first novel, *She Came to Stay*, aptly illustrates her own dictum that 'literature is born when something in life goes slightly adrift'. Like the majority of her novels it draws closely on personal experiences, vividly portraying the conflicts and jealousy she herself experienced during Sartre's involvement with Olga. *She Came to Stay* is set in Bohemian Paris; the characters have occupations, backgrounds, and preoccupations similar to those she describes in the second volume of her autobiography, *The Prime of Life*. The same familiar world provides the context of her two subsequent major novels, *The Blood of Others* and *The Mandarins*, which again variously draw on situations and events documented in her autobiographical accounts. But although there are close parallels between de Beauvoir's novels and her own life, there is a transformation and commitment in her fiction that is very far from the unreflexive reportage of personal experiences and events. Experience has to be reconstructed, interpreted, and explained. It is the nature of the underlying principles of this reconstruction that is the central theme of this chapter, for unlike the work of many other novelists, de Beauvoir's fiction is marked, in much the same way as her non-fiction, by a concern to illustrate and elaborate what she sees as certain key philosophical problems. Thus human experience and the problems of personal life are used to illustrate ethical and moral problems; like Sartre, de Beauvoir used literature, and generally the novel, to show how these problems are created and how they might be resolved. The dilemmas posed by de Beauvoir (particularly in *She Came to Stay* and *The Mandarins*) were all known to or personally experienced by her, yet – although she appears as a character in her own novels (for example as Anne in *The Mandarins*) – she does not write from the point of view of a single character, so that what emerges is in no sense a subjective novel. Indeed, a function of de Beauvoir's fiction seems to be to objectify the problems of her own life: in the retelling of the strains and stresses of her own emotional life she overcomes them. Through rational understanding, and rationality, the irrational world is made safe.

There is, therefore, an intensely personal element in de Beauvoir's work, in that she uses both the experiences of her own life and her experience of the world, as the data from which she constructs fiction and non-fiction alike. In this she answers the feminist call that women should speak of their own lives, but of course the curious and fascinating element in de Beauvoir's work is the way in which she interprets her own experiences as a woman. Far from simply letting her own voice speak, she constructs novels and philosophy from her emotional and social history, and in so doing makes extensive use of the rationality, the logic, and the philosophical systems of the male world. De Beauvoir's work therefore offers to the reader a rich amalgam of influences: lived experience of the world as a heterosexual woman, full participation from an early age in an intellectual world largely dominated by men, and a self-conscious determination to escape from her background and the domestic world of women. Whether de Beauvoir's education diminished or enriched her understanding of the world of women must remain a debatable point: on the one hand it could be said that de Beauvoir imposed on the female world male values and standards, on the other that she potentially released women and their experiences from passive subjectivity. Certainly, at no point in her adolescence or early maturity did she question the value of the education that she was receiving. Further, the promise of the rational understanding of the world which education offered was its sufficient vindication.

It had been de Beauvoir's intention, from her adolescence, to construct for herself a world which, in contrast to the petit-bourgeois society of her parents, she could respect and accept. *The Prime of Life* outlines the many conversations which she and Sartre had in which they outlined their future way of life. From an early age de Beauvoir had detested the political and moral views of her family, and had little sympathy with the conservative, nationalistic beliefs of her class. Not for her the narrow-minded chauvinism or moral hypocrisy of the French petit bourgeois; her life was to be cosmopolitan and committed to the pursuit of freedom and truth. Above all else, her life was to be self-conscious: one of de Beauvoir's greatest fears in *Memoirs of a Dutiful Daughter* and *The Prime of Life* seems to have been the possibility of following blindly the dictates of conventional morality. The moral of the failure to choose a morality is implied in the account of the death of Elizabeth Mabille and the decline into drunken futility of her cousin Jacques: to fail to choose is to relinquish one's freedom and consequently one's capacity for action. This moral – with its accompaniment of the fear of refusing choice – dominates de Beauvoir's fiction and is very much the message which she wishes to impart to her readers. But the problem for many of her readers is not the assumption that individuals should choose their fate, but the nature of the relationship between an individual choice and other people. De Beauvoir's call for an active individual morality must, therefore, be seen in the context of her views on social and political life in general.

Merleau-Ponty once described Sartre's form of socialist commitment as a 'conception of freedom that allows only for sudden interventions into the world', and de Beauvoir's political actions largely followed this pattern.[1] Her commitments were absolute, and often demanded great personal courage, but the pattern of her political interventions was that of identification with particular causes rather than with movements and parties. Despite the political activism that was to characterize their lives after the Second World War it is apparent that before the war both Sartre and de Beauvoir were mostly concerned with questions concerning their personal lives. They were far from politically ignorant or dismissive of such events as the Spanish Civil War or the Popular Front in France, but equally they were not, as de Beauvoir puts it, 'actively for anything'. Their politics were essentially anarchist, their ideas those of rebellion rather than revolution. Despite the contacts they both had with individuals who were politically committed (for example Paul Nizan, the author of *Aden-Arabie* and *Les Chiens de Garde*), neither was drawn into the ranks of political activism. Two instances in de Beauvoir's autobiography illustrate vividly her attitudes in this period. First, she recalls a conversation she had with Simone Weil, while both were students at the Sorbonne:

'I don't know how the conversation got started; she decided in no uncertain terms that only one thing mattered in the world today: the Revolution which would feed all the starving people of the

earth. I retorted, no less peremptorily, that the problem was not
to make men happy but to find the reason for their existence. She
looked me up and down: "It's easy to see you've never gone
hungry," she snapped.'

(MDD, 239)

Reflecting on this attitude at the beginning of the Second World War,
de Beauvoir looks at herself and her values, and writes:

'Hitherto my sole concern had been to enrich my personal life and
learn the art of converting it into words. Little by little I had
abandoned the solipsism and illusory autonomy I cherished as a
girl of twenty; though I had come to recognise the fact of other
people's existence, it was still my individual relationships with
separate people that mattered most to me, and I still yearned
fiercely for happiness. Then, suddenly, History burst over me,
and I dissolved into fragments. I woke to find myself scattered
over the four quarters of the globe, linked by every nerve in me to
each and every individual. All my ideas and values were turned
upside down; even the pursuit of happiness lost its importance
. . . . when I ceased to regard my life as an autonomous and
self-sufficient project, I was obliged to rediscover my links with a
universe the very face of which I had forgotten.'

(PL, 369)

The universe which de Beauvoir claimed to have forgotten in the
1930s was, of course, largely a world in which she wished to have no
part. In emancipating herself from her home and background, she had
found that to a certain extent she could reject that bourgeois world and
its values. Her life since leaving the Sorbonne had not been without its
difficulties, but for all the unconventionality of some aspects of that life,
both Sartre and de Beauvoir had been able 'to defy the conventions
with impunity'. As she wrote:

'We had each in our own way been pursuing a dream – as Sartre
has suggested in *The Reprieve*, we were all living an unreal life
centred upon the preservation of the peace. No one possessed the
necessary equipment to group the over-all pattern of this new
world then coming about, which could not be understood at all
except in its totality. Nevertheless I carried my rejection of
History and its dangers to extraordinary lengths!'

(PL, 363–64B)

But in a sense this rejection of 'History' was understandable; after all, 'History' did not impinge on de Beauvoir during the 1930s in any direct social or material sense. The privilege of her position as an *agrégée* of the Sorbonne was such that *de facto* she belonged to an élite group. Her friendships brought her into contact with French intellectual circles, and, given de Beauvoir's access to this network and her residence in Paris after 1938, it is only surprising that *The Prime of Life* contains relatively little mention of contemporary political and intellectual life. Certainly, films, books, and the major political events of the time are documented but active engagement with intellectual life is very much a post-war phenomenon. An instance of this shift in attitude is de Beauvoir's view of Sartre's journalistic exercises: she describes his contributions in the 1930s to *La Nouvelle Revue Française* and *Europe* (both leading journals of the French literary left) as 'a frittering away of his talents' but during the war she actively supported his work for *Combat* and, more significantly, played a major part in the foundation in 1945 of *Les Temps Modernes*.

These instances of de Beauvoir's increasing move towards political intervention between 1939 and 1945 indicate the way in which she was gradually coming to confront some of the problems implicit in the moral system that she and Sartre had fashioned for themselves since their days as students. It is apparent from both *Memoirs of a Dutiful Daughter* and *The Prime of Life* that both were dissatisfied with the education they had received. Sartre took himself off from the major part of the student body, forming a small, exclusive group which 'had no truck with anybody else; they only attended certain lectures and always sat apart from the rest of us'. This group, consisting of Sartre, Nizan, and 'Herbaud' (a pseudonym used by de Beauvoir for a friend of that period), was more than socially exclusive and disdainful of the other students, it was also actively in revolt against the kind of philosophy then taught at the Sorbonne and the *École Normale*. The content of the syllabus of these august institutions, indeed the central issues of French philosophy at the time, have been described by H. Stuart Hughes in *The Obstructed Path* as amounting to an 'official' view of the world:

'Neither among the English nor among the Germans did the classical tradition prompt the dominant style of thought. England had no single "official" philosopher; Germany had Kant, but by the twentieth century the Kantian tradition had been interpreted so variously as to remain only the vaguest point of reference – and besides, few pedagogues aimed to teach children to write like Kant. In France, in contrast, Descartes had

for nearly three centuries supplied a ready-made style of thought
and of expression; Cartesianism suffused the intellectual
atmosphere so thoroughly that much of the time it went
unnoticed. The French not only possessed an official philosopher;
they had in the Cartesian tradition a pass-key that did service for
literature and social thought alike.'   (Hughes 1968: 4)

Now it has always been an apparently irresistible temptation for
intellectual historians to produce grand-scale generalizations about the
nature of a particular culture or intellectual tradition. The debate
between Perry Anderson and E. P. Thompson on the deficiencies or
strengths of English letters and politics is just one such example. But
whether or not Hughes's remarks on France are accepted as the whole
truth about Gallic intellectual habits in the 1930s, it is apparent from
the testimony of the French themselves that whatever the excellences of
French academic training, pluralism was not one of its features. Nor
has it ever been: in Régis Debray's recent attack on the French 'star'
system of intellectual life one point to which he frequently returns is
the narrowness of the French Academy; its concerns and its reading
have long been inflexibly parochial (Debray 1979).

So what is often held by Francophiles to be one of the great cultures
of the world (if not the greatest) has been found by many of its students
to be seriously deficient. Certainly, for Sartre, de Beauvoir, and other
critics of their generation, intellectual innovation lay elsewhere:
predominantly in Germany and the United States. In *The Prime of Life*
de Beauvoir records that Sartre spent a year in Berlin (1933–34),
following in the footsteps of Raymond Aron as a postgraduate student
at the French Institute there. De Beauvoir also writes enthusiastically
of the interest she and Sartre shared during the 1930s in the culture of
the United States, for across the Atlantic was an entirely novel
civilization, producing jazz, films, and a way of life foreign to anything
then known in Europe and France.

In contrast to these Germanic and North American excitements, France
was producing little in the early 1930s that could be described as novel
or encouraging. Nor was it entirely surprising that the academic and
cultural life of the country was limited to a small coterie in Paris: the
rest of the society remained predominantly agricultural, non-urban,
and largely composed of peasant farmers. In turning elsewhere for
intellectual novelty de Beauvoir and Sartre followed the pattern of the
French avant-garde of their generation. Among the small group of
like-minded students who, with Sartre, opposed the orthodoxy of the
French Academy, Sartre and Nizan represented two different kinds of

response to the dominant ideology: Nizan embraced Marxism, while Sartre was preoccupied with developing a moral system that allowed the individual an absolute centrality. From an early age contemptuous of universalistic explanations, and general laws and concepts, Sartre envisaged a world-wide system of intelligence centred upon the concrete – and therefore upon the individual, since only the individual entity has any real existence. The problem with this system, as Nizan and another of Sartre's contemporaries, the Marxist Politzer, were quick to point out, was precisely the isolated autonomy it gave to the individual. In rejecting both Marxism and psychoanalysis Sartre allowed each individual to be considered as having been born *tabula rasa* with the potential of becoming a being of both perfect rationality and perfect freedom, unconstrained by either personal or social history.

But none of these criticisms prevented Sartre, with de Beauvoir's active assistance and encouragement, from working towards the formulation of a moral system that could allow individuals the freedom to define and control their own actions. What was to emerge from these ideals was Sartre's version of existentialism: a philosophical system often credited to Sartre, but in terms of its origins actually derived, as Sartre's own work makes clear, from the writings of Kierkegaard, Nietzsche and Heidegger. All these figures were preoccupied, as Sartre and de Beauvoir were to be, with achieving authenticity in human actions, with liberating individuals from the constraints and distortions of generalized social norms and values, and with both forcing and allowing human beings to make choices founded on their own interpretations and experience of situations. Within this sytem therefore there can be no 'musts' or 'shoulds', no invocation of absolute duty or responsibility, only the confrontation by all individuals separately of their own responsibilities, to themselves and their individual values. Consciousness must be raised to the point of self-consciousness, the accepted must be questioned, and the boundaries challenged. Or, as Nietzsche has been quoted as saying: 'The secret of the greatest fruitfulness and the greatest enjoyment of existence is to live dangerously.' Sartre clearly took the same view of the proper way to live, and in *Memoirs of a Dutiful Daughter* de Beauvoir recalls that the young Sartre intended to make 'tremendous journeys: in Constantinople he would fraternize with the dock-workers; he would get blind drunk with pimps and white-slaves in sinks of iniquity' (MDD, 341).

That Sartre did none of these things, but lived a life of consistent normality and commitment to hard work, is of course no reflection on the strength of the philosophical system that he elaborated. Yet Sartre's exhortations to others, his whole concept of being and of an authentic existence, were based on the rejection of the normal habits and assumptions of everyday life. What de Beauvoir was to realize – and here a significant shift occurs between her early and mature work – was that men have more freedom than women to make those crucial existential choices. In *She Came to Stay* and *The Blood of Others* the sexes are seen as equal in their capacity to make existential choices, yet only a few years later – in *The Second Sex* – de Beauvoir has recognized the constraints on women that inhibit their full participation in the world. Men, she argues in *The Second Sex*, can assert their will in the world and then be judged by their actions and decisions. On the other hand the limitations of women's situation are such that they are offered few opportunities to act, they are merely handed given social roles (as wife, mother, mistress) and then judged according to their performance within these categories, categories which are themselves structured by male interests and activities. The escape which de Beauvoir proposes for women from this subjectivity is through the wholesale rejection of traditional female roles: the way to freedom is to follow the path already forged by men. The limitations of this blueprint for emancipation are discussed in later chapters; the point here is that it took de Beauvoir some time even to acknowledge the different constraints under which men and women live: during the 1930s she had endorsed and encouraged all Sartre's efforts towards the elaboration of an existential morality without apparently ever questioning its different implications for men and women.

Indeed, *The Second Sex* was years away when Sartre was developing his early work on morality and ethics. In the 1930s Sartre and, to a certain extent, de Beauvoir were concerned to demonstrate ethical problems of human behaviour through literature. During this decade the most important works Sartre published were *Nausea* and short stories (*Intimacy*, *The Wall*, *The Room*, *Erostratus*, and *The Childhood of a Leader*). Philosophy was represented by *Sketch for a Theory of the Emotions*, *Imagination*, and *The Legend of Truth*, all of which have been described as having 'little more than purely documentary interest for they are truly "pen exercises", rather than original works' (Meszaros 1979: 79). It was not until 1943, with the publication of *Being and Nothingness*,[2] that Sartre completed a detailed outline of his philosophical system. It did not make an immediate impact; indeed, so complex and lengthy were its arguments, and so apparently distant from the immediate concerns of everyday life, that it passed the German censor without difficulty and raised no eyebrows with the occupying authorities (in part perhaps because throughout the book Sartre fully acknowledged his debt to the German philosophical tradition, in particular Husserl, Heidegger, and Hegel).

The central, organizing premise of *Being and Nothingness* is that there exists a fundamental distinction between consciousness, which Sartre describes as 'for-itself' (*pour soi*), and the phenomenal world (including its derived consciousness) which he described as 'in-itself' (*en soi*). Consciousness that is 'for-itself' is consciousness that is radically free;[3] it has the ability to assert an individual perception of the world and to defy habits and conventions that seem to limit the possibilities of human action. Yet action for Sartre is not conceived of in terms of attempts at transformations of the universe, or even of more limited personal adventures into the unknown and the unorthodox. Rather it is a concept of action which emphasizes the active possibilities of rejection of the conventional expectations of the world. As Sartre explained in *Being and Nothingness*, the world is structured by moral codes and norms: every culture and society expects of its citizens a certain acceptance of these premises, and those who reject them are labelled bad or even mad. But accepting social norms carries the cost of acting in what Sartre describes as bad faith – a state in which individuals commit what for Sartre is the gravest sin in the list of possible evils, that of denying their own capacity for choice. To follow a course of action because of guilt, remorse, social restraint, or responsibility to others is to reject what Sartre sees as the most precious of human capacities, the possibility of freedom.

Thus stated, Sartre's moral system recalls nothing more or less than the morality of the free market. If we are all 'condemned to be free' and have a fundamental responsibility to assert our capacity for freedom and choice against the taken-for-granted moral universe then we might assume that it is acceptable for individuals to follow their own inclinations, regardless of the interests of other people. It is at this point in Sartre's reasoning that we encounter that crucial figure in the existentialist system: the other. It is also the point at which de Beauvoir's work takes up the issues and problems posed by Sartre's system. Although de Beauvoir published an essay on existentialist ethics (*Pour une morale de l'ambiguité*) she did not, like Sartre, develop a fully articulated philosophical and ethical system. But what she did do in her first three novels (especially in *She Came to Stay* and *The Blood of Others*) was to give human reality to the problems raised by existentialism. To a large extent, of course, this is also true of Sartre. *The Roads to Freedom* and the majority of his plays are all illustrative of the dilemmas confronting human beings in situations in which they have to make moral choices. But the characters who face the moral dilemmas posed by de Beauvoir in her fiction (and by Sartre in *The Age of Reason*) all have a characteristic in contradiction with the existentialist ideal of a perfectly free individual: they are constrained in their actions by their emotional involvements with others. The ties between people – and particularly the tie between the subject and the other – are thus a crucial element in de Beauvoir's fiction, for she recognizes that human beings do both love others and feel guilty about causing them pain, and yet at the same time long for a state of emotional autonomy in which their actions will not be shaped by those feelings.

It is this sentiment called 'love' that causes the greatest difficulty for Sartre and de Beauvoir. If we love, then the question arises of how to prevent emotions from becoming a constraint on the liberty of ourselves and others. A cardinal existentialist sin would be to say that 'Love means asking the other to limit his or her behaviour'. The likelihood that people will do this, that relations between men and women will become circumscribed and fall into those conventional patterns so despised by Sartre and de Beauvoir, is a constant theme of their fiction. For both, sexual relationships and strong personal ties are beset by fears about constraint. In Sartre's work in particular there is a crucial additional dimension to this fear – a fear of the flesh:

> 'This metaphysical disgust could on occasion extend to the entire corporeal aspect of existence; at one point in *Being and Nothingness* Sartre referred almost casually to the "nauseous character of all flesh".'

And as Hughes goes on to point out:

> 'As the mythic carriers of fleshly values, women thus became automatically suspect: Sartre's critics have repeatedly drawn attention to the harsh treatment he dealt them in his plays and novels, where they figured as soft, damp, porous, and once even as a "swamp". If the flesh (or life, or existence) was dense and viscous – in short, – female – the intellect was hard and sharp and male.'

> (Hughes 1968: 82)

De Beauvoir does not admit to an explicit hostility to the flesh (although her remarks on her discovery of her own capacity for sexual desire in *The Prime of Life* come close to suspicion and dislike of the body) but there is some evidence, in both her fiction and her non-fiction, that she did share with Sartre a fear of the ties that physical love could create. To give precedence to love and personal ties is perceived by de Beauvoir as especially dangerous for women. The difference between Sartre and de Beauvoir here is not that one accepts and the other denies ties of the flesh but that Sartre sees men as trapped by women while de Beauvoir sees women as all too likely to imprison themselves.

These underlying themes, and the explicit concern with existential choices and dilemmas are to be found throughout de Beauvoir's fiction, but most particularly in the three 'existentialist' novels: *She Came to Stay* (1943), *The Blood of Others* (1945), and *All Men Are Mortal* (1946). In this period de Beauvoir also published two brief essays on existentialist ethics: *Pyrrhus et Cinéas* (1944) and *Pour une morale de l'ambiguité* (1947). In all these works a view of freedom as a state which human beings construct for themselves is quite clearly stated or implied: people may live in difficult or constraining circumstances, but the choice between freedom and constraint is still seen as possible for all human beings. In *She Came to Stay* and *The Blood of Others* a message of unmitigated individualism is communicated. Despite the fact that *The Blood of Others* takes place in occupied Paris, and is often described as a 'Resistance' novel, the characters are all presented as having a tremendous capacity for individual moral decisions. The last paragraph of *She Came to Stay* summarizes, with great force, the significance which de Beauvoir clearly envisaged at the time of individual, freely chosen acts:

> 'Alone. She had acted alone: as alone as in death one day Pierre
> would know. But even his cognizance of this deed would be
> merely external. No one could condemn or absolve her. Her act
> was her very own. "It is I who will it". It was her own will which
> was being accomplished, now nothing at all separated her from
> herself. She had at last made a choice. She had chosen herself.'
>
> (SCS, 416)

Many of the limitations and shortcomings of existentialism as a guide to morality, let alone social life, are illustrated by this conclusion, and indeed by much of the action and the motivation of the characters in *She Came to Stay*. The novel concerns three central characters – Pierre, Françoise, and Xavière. For years Pierre and Françoise have had a happy, rewarding, and stable relationship. This is jeopardized by the arrival of an outsider, Xavière. The plot is, of course, based on the real-life trio of Sartre, de Beauvoir, and Olga except that the novel does not just imitate life, it somewhat melodramatically alters it, in that the fictional de Beauvoir (Françoise) eventually kills Xavière. The novel invites us to believe that Françoise had no real alternative; Xavière is destroying a relationship which is of immense value to Pierre and Françoise. Only Françoise, less attracted to Xavière than Pierre is, has the necessary perception to realize that the situation demands resolution and alteration. But how is the alteration to be achieved? The pact of semi-fidelity which Françoise and Pierre have concluded (again we find echoes of Sartre and de Beauvoir) does not allow for the exclusion of others. Indeed, it is quite clearly a matter of some pride to both Françoise and Pierre that their relationship should have room for Xavière. Both of them, initially, would regard it as absurd to say that Xavière must be excluded from their lives, on the grounds that she is a threat to their stability. Neither would acknowledge 'stability' as a value; in this particular instance both would argue that if either was to exclude Xavière from their lives on the grounds that she was a disruptive influence, then that party would be guilty of oppressing the other by erecting false, institutional, values about 'stability' and 'permanence'. The relationship between Pierre and Françoise must be one, therefore, in which each party freely consents and chooses to be with the other.

Probably only those with lurking sympathies for sexual slavery would challenge that view about the proper basis for human relationships. However, as Pierre and Françoise (and Sartre and de Beauvoir) were to discover, this blueprint for existence is not quite adequate for all situations which confront human beings; it fails to cover the common situation in which one member of a couple is attracted to a third party. The problem then becomes one of the extent to which the expression and realization of that attraction becomes oppressive to the excluded partner. He or she might well protest, as indeed Françoise and de Beauvoir initially do, that no problem exists: jealousy and hierarchies of emotional commitment are features of a bourgeois world, cultural constructs which have no place among human beings who are in daily control of their own moral fate. Unfortunately, both Françoise and de Beauvoir are to discover that recognizing a culturally constructed emotion or desire is quite another thing from being able to liberate themselves from it. Even if we assume that the difficulties which de Beauvoir and Françoise face in their triadic relationships are not as simple or as straightforward as being merely about jealousy or exclusion from the emotional life of a previously faithful partner, it is possible to see that for both there is an intolerable gap between the emotional reality of their situation, and the understanding and guidance available to them from the philosophical system which they espoused. Existentialism, with its emphasis on the need for each individual to construct his or her own moral reality, was no help in a situation in which the freely chosen actions of one party oppressed another.

This difficulty was, of course, recognized by both Sartre and de Beauvoir. Neither of them failed to see that unlimited human freedom was likely to oppress the weak and the vulnerable. But having conceded that point, they still had to answer the question of how they would ensure that in choosing to be free in particular ways, human beings do not act oppressively. The innate anarchy of their views in the 1930s led both Sartre and de Beauvoir to reject all formal, institutional constraints on freedom. What Sartre was eventually to put in the place of bourgeois law and order, and moral and social convention, was the concept of bad faith: the state in which an individual acts knowing that his or her actions will oppress others. If, therefore, a lover acts in bad faith, that lover acts in such a way as to deny the freedom, and the autonomy, of the other party. Thus in *Pour une morale de l'ambiguité* de Beauvoir argued that:

> 'To love him (another) genuinely is to love him in his otherness and in that freedom by which he escapes. One renounces being in order that there may be that being which one is not . . . no existence can be validly fulfilled if it is limited to itself.'
>
> (EA, 67)

According to these guiding principles it is only to be expected that Françoise will make no claims upon Pierre, and will allow him to develop his friendship with Xavière in the way which he thinks is most appropriate. Equally, de Beauvoir was bound to make no demands on Sartre: if she did, then she would be betraying the principle which she espoused in the passage quoted above, that love, in her view, means never making claims.

Inevitably, western culture being what it is, and its idea of love and sexual relationships having the form that it does, the abstract principle is unequal to the reality of human experience and expectation. When de Beauvoir writes of a phenomenon known as 'love' she is writing of a sentiment which she barely examines at all in any critical sense. Thus she accepts as given the existence of a feeling between, and towards, individuals which has a certain false homogeneity about it. Her auto-biography demonstrates clearly that what she felt for Sartre, Algren, and Lanzmann was something she called 'love'. What she does not even consider is that in each of those cases, the original nature of the 'love' was about individualized heterosexual attraction: an attraction represented, and defined, both by a certain kind of personality in each of the particular cases and by the possibility of the fulfilment of particular needs at a particular point. Sartre, it is reasonable to suppose, represented the liberating powers of the intellect, the person who could illuminate and strengthen an already existing desire to escape from the confines of bourgeois life. Both Algren and Lanzmann fulfilled, as de Beauvoir admits in *Force of Circumstance*, certain needs at certain points in her life. For example, in 1947, finding her self alone in New York, with Sartre asking her to postpone her return to France, she wanted a man who could be 'hers', a person who could, we must suppose, give her emotional and sexual reassurance, at a moment of acute emotional insecurity. That Algren would fall as much 'in love' with her as she did with him was a matter, eventually, of anguish to them both. In choosing to begin, and to remain in, a relationship with Claude Lanzmann, de Beauvoir again speaks of 'love', but few readers of her autobiography can avoid noting that in embarking on this relationship de Beauvoir did so with a man who represented no real threat to her relationship with Sartre. What we might also note about all these relationships is that de Beauvoir 'loved' the men concerned perhaps less because of their individual characteristics than because of her own needs at particular points in her life. Thus in early maturity she needed a man who could guide her out of petit-bourgeois life – Sartre filled that role just as much as Algren and Lanzmann filled her later needs for emotional support and physical affection. That we do not love freely, but because of the very powerful constraints of our own needs and biographies is only briefly considered, even though the issue raises fascinating questions about the needs of the sexes for each other.

The problems that de Beauvoir's somewhat conventional and uncritical attitude to heterosexual love raised are nowhere better illustrated than in her own account of her affair with Nelson Algren. The relationship began out of what can only be described as mixed motives: alone in New York, de Beauvoir was asked by Sartre to postpone her return to Paris because his lover (the woman always referred to as 'M') wished to prolong her stay in Paris, and he did not wish de Beauvoir to return until 'M' had departed. (This attitude is in itself revealing: since Sartre and de Beauvoir did not share a domestic space, 'M' can hardly have been said to be occupying the matrimonial home – nevertheless Sartre's ideas on emotional space, the other, and the boundaries of propriety did not allow the most significant women in his life to be in the same city at the same time.) Thus forced to spend additional time in the United States de Beauvoir writes that she '(had) had enough of being a tourist; I wanted to walk about on the arm of a man who, temporarily, would be mine' (FC. 126). Alone, and probably lonely, de Beauvoir telephones Algren and suggests a meeting.

From then on, accounts of what happened next diverge. The beginning of the affair is described by de Beauvoir thus: 'I called Algren. "Can you come here?" I asked him. He couldn't; but would

like very much to see me in Chicago. I arranged for him to meet me at
the airport' (FC, 126)

Algren's account is rather different:

> 'the phone rang and someone hollered into it, screeched
> something and I hung up. I said "wrong number." I had
> something cooking. No sooner than I had got back to the stove,
> the phone rang again and I got the same hoarse screech and I did
> this three times. The last time I hung up I just said, "Wrong
> number", and bang! About half an hour later the phone rang and
> a very clear voice said, "would you mind holding the phone for a
> minute, don't hang up for just a minute, there's a party here
> would like to speak to you." So then I listened and next a heavily
> accented French voice was saying that her name was, ah, ah,
> something. I didn't quite catch it. I said, "Where are you at, I'll
> come down." "Leetle Cafe," she told me, "in Palmer House." I'd
> never hear of it. I'd heard of the Palmer House all right, but not of
> the Leetle Cafe. When I got down there all I saw was "*Le Petit
> Cafe*". She wasn't taking any chance on my understanding it
> looked like. Then I saw this woman coming wiz copy of leetle
> magazine – *Partisan Review*. That threw me off. I leaped to the
> conclusion she'd been sent by Mary McCarthy. I don't want a
> date with Mary McCarthy even by surrogate. I decided to think
> this over.'

(Donohue 1963: 180–81)

This rather unpropitious beginning did not prevent Algren and de
Beauvoir from becoming lovers, and very much involved with each
other. In *Force of Circumstance*, de Beauvoir describes her time with
Algren and their travels with obvious nostalgia. But the most vivid
presentation of the romance is to be found in *The Mandarins* in the
portrayal of the affair between Anne and Lewis Brogan: an affair which
de Beauvoir always admitted was a largely autobiographical recollec-
tion of her own affair with Algren. *The Mandarins* contains passages
describing the most intense emotional experiences between Anne (de
Beauvoir) and Lewis (Algren). What is remarkable about some of the
descriptions is the extraordinarily conventional way in which they
describe physical love between men and women, and the nature of
sexual and emotional attraction. Consider, for example, this passage
from *The Mandarins*, in which de Beauvoir is describing Anne's reaction
to her first night with Brogan:

> 'The warmth of his voice reassured me . . . . There was no need to
> be upset; he was caressing my hair, speaking gently, simple

words, slipping an old copper ring on my finger. . . . Nothing was asked of me; I had only to be exactly what I was and a man's desire transformed me into a miracle of perfection.'

(TM, 424)

Or an equally emotionally charged passage describing Anne's reaction when Lewis asks her to stay with him:

'He had hurled those words at me with such violence that I fell into his arms. I kissed his eyes, his lips, my mouth went down along his chest. His smell, his warmth made me dizzy as with drink and I felt my life leaving me, my old life with its worries, its worries, its weariness, its worn-out memories. Lewis held a totally new woman against him. I moaned, and not only with pleasure, but with happiness.'

(TM, 434)

The moaning, the surrender of female autonomy to male desire, and the claiming of a woman by a ring, are all quite traditional features of romantic fiction. Women are expected to 'surrender' to men, to experience in the physical expression of heterosexuality a kind of general anaesthetic from which they emerge 'complete' or 'at one' with the beloved. The style and the terminology of these passages are therefore very close to all those conventional romantic novels which de Beauvoir must inevitably despise. But the essential issue is not the style of the passages, but the underlying assumption which de Beauvoir makes: that shared, and desired, sexuality between men and women involves feelings of commitment and exclusivity. De Beauvoir does not always ask us to connect sexuality and commitment (indeed she contrasts the cold promiscuity of Anne's daughter Nadine with the warmth of Anne's feelings for Lewis) but she does ask us to accept that women, at least, find in sex with men they love a feeling of transcendence and surrender to male sexual power and desire.

But sexuality, however intensely pleasurable, remains problematic, both for Anne and de Beauvoir. For de Beauvoir and Algren, it cemented and enriched their relationship, but at the same time it brought about the relationship's destruction, for it created desires of permanence and stability that could not be reconciled with de Beauvoir's existing life with Sartre. The affair ended unhappily: de Beauvoir could not give up Sartre, and Algren wrote subsequently that he felt betrayed by de Beauvoir, who, in his view, had entered into the relationship with him knowing from the start that it had no future. As numerous other lovers, both in fiction and in fact, have discovered, a love affair has to have either a future or an end. In a biting review of *Force of Circumstance*, Algren writes of the pact that Sartre and de Beauvoir concluded:

'Procurers are more honest than philosophers. They name this How-about-a-quickie-kid gambit as "chippying" and regard the middle class woman who indulges herself in it with less respect than they give the fireship who shoves a shiv into a faithless lover's anatomy.'

(Algren 1965)

Thus despite the many happy times and affectionate intimacies which de Beauvoir and Algren shared, the relationship ended unhappily: Algren bitter about what he felt had been a consistent deceit and de Beauvoir depressed and unhappy at the loss of an emotionally and sexually active relationship. In an intensely charged passage of *The Mandarins* describing the first days that de Beauvoir (Anne) and Algren (Lewis) spend together, we are given some idea of exactly what the relationship meant to de Beauvoir:

'I was naked, I was naked and I felt no uneasiness. His eyes could not hurt me; he didn't judge me. From the top of my head to my toes, his hands learned me by heart. Again I said, "I love your hands." "You love them?" "All evening I wondered whether I would feel them on my body."

"You will feel them all night", he said. Suddenly he was neither awkward nor modest. His lust transfigured me; I who for so long had had no taste, no form, I again possessed breasts, a belly, a sex; flesh. I was nourishing like bread, I had smells like earth. It was so miraculous that I didn't think of measuring time or place. I only know that when we finally drifted off, one could hear the feeble trills of dawn.'

(TM, 423)

Compared to the life de Beauvoir had left in Paris, in which Sartre had made no secret of his affection for 'M' and had therefore excluded de Beauvoir from his personal, emotional life, the attractions of the United States and Algren can hardly have been less than overwhelming.

But set against these rich, new possibilities there lay the constant problem of old ties and old loyalties. The vows that Sartre and de Beauvoir had made to each other had not been of permanent emotional exclusivity or monogamy, but they had been promises of life-long commitment – the 'essential love' which de Beauvoir describes in *The*

Prime of Life. When others intruded into this relationship, both Sartre and de Beauvoir were to discover that existentialist principles about freedom were inadequate, and indeed irrelevant, to the problems resulting from their relations with others. Certainly, both de Beauvoir and Sartre 'allowed' each other to enter into relationships with others, but what existed as a constant constraint on the development of these relationships was the understanding between de Beauvoir and Sartre. In a passage in *Force of Circumstances* in which she comments on Sartre's affair with 'M' de Beauvoir writes of some of the problems of the definitions and limits of love:

> 'if he loved her, how could he bear not to see her for months at a time? He listened to her complaints with remorse; he felt he was to blame. Of course he had warned her that there could be no question of his making a life with her. But by saying he loved her, he gave the lie to that warning, for – especially in the eyes of women – love triumphs over every obstacle. M. was not entirely in the wrong. Love's promises express the passion of a moment only; restrictions and reservations are no more binding; in every case, the truth of the present sweeps all pledges imperiously before it.'

(FC, 127)

The same reflections, it is impossible not to think, might well apply to de Beauvoir herself: both she and Sartre showed, at least in some of their dealings with others, a grave disregard for the freedom of those individuals, in that they (Sartre and de Beauvoir) knew the limits on any new relationships from the start and thus trapped the others in situations which were already curtailed and limited. De Beauvoir and Sartre certainly did not exclude 'others' from their lives but the terms on which those 'others' would enter their lives has already been set, and set in ways which they could not alter.

De Beauvoir's reflections on the 'other' and on the nature of morality are not, however, developed solely in her fiction. *She Came to Stay* represents de Beauvoir's first exploration of the problems of loyalty and freedom but in the essays *Pyrrhus et Cinéas* and *Pour une morale de l'ambiguité* de Beauvoir outlines her views on morality and ethics. Neither essay devotes a great deal of attention to the material and historical circumstances that may create constraints on freedom and moral choice, but they both suggest a world of complete freedom in which people do not make the best choices in difficult circumstances (and may therefore make the least damaging, rather than the best moral choice) but make absolutely good or bad decisions in situations in which *only* the moral limits and constraints of the situation are relevant.

Both *Pyrrhus et Cinéas* and *Pour une morale de l'ambiguité* are essentially concerned with ethics, and both were immediately defined by the critics as existentialist statements. According to de Beauvoir's analysis in *Pour une morale de l'ambiguité*, there are two contrasting attitudes towards moral issues – to the question of how to live – for the great majority of people. For the first group, those who have what she describes as an 'infantile morality', there are no ethical questions to be asked, let alone answered, since for them ethics already exist, in a pre-packaged form, in law and social convention. What society tells people to do, and what people in society generally do, assumes for this group the status of moral law. The second group of human beings de Beauvoir describes as those with the ethics of the 'adventurer'. She uses two examples to illustrate what she means by an adventurer: the sexual philanderer Don Juan and the colonialist Cortez. Both, from different motivations and for different reasons, set out to oppress the vulnerable and the weak. Both were quite indifferent to the existence, the needs, or the interests of others, and were concerned with other people solely to the extent that those others could gratify their own interests.

Since the morality (or lack of morality) of Don Juan and Cortez is as unacceptable to de Beauvoir as that of the slavish conformist, she has to develop an alternative morality. She does so by arguing that moral laws must come from within each individual and not from society. Don Juan and Cortez are, she suggests, as conformist in their own ways as anyone who is too frightened to break a social code, since both are conforming to social patterns, albeit in a more aggressive and extrovert way than the passive servant of social rules. Thus Don Juan is obeying that social convention which states that men must pursue women sexually; Cortez is accepting the premise of bourgeois society that profit must be pursued to the fullest extent, regardless of the human consequences. But in saying that people must develop their own morality and reject the conformist patterns which predict and regulate the behaviour of Cortez, Don Juan, and every slave of convention, de Beauvoir has to answer the question of where that morality is to come from, and, most important of all, the kind of premises that it is to be based upon. She answers her own question by arguing that a part, a most important part, of each human being's very humanity is his or her capacity for liberty and freedom. Hence at this stage in the argument innate characteristics of human beings intrude: in this case the capacity of men and women to recognize freedom, and value its preservation. Since all human beings possess this capability, it is essential for the preservation of their own liberty – in fact their own humanity – that they should fight to preserve the liberty of others. Unless we can recognize the liberty and the right to freedom of others, we are, de Beauvoir asserts, denying a part of our being. An authentic moral code is one that takes into account two facets of human existence: that people are both individuals and social beings.

The conflicts between one's own desire for freedom and the rights of other people to freedom constitute the major theme of Simone de Beauvoir's existentialist novels: *She Came to Stay*, *All Men Are Mortal*, and *The Blood of Others*. The problems raised in *She Came to Stay* have already been discussed earlier in this chapter, but the chief issue of that novel – how an individual can pursue his or her own desires without injuring others – is echoed in *All Men Are Mortal* and *The Blood of Others*. In *All Men Are Mortal* (a novel which concerns an Italian nobleman of the thirteenth century who drinks an elixir which turns him into a time traveller) the major concern of the novel is to demonstrate that indifference is a denial of freedom. From numerous points of view the novel is unsatisfactory: the nobleman (Fosca) is quite obviously either most unlucky or most inept, since his time travelling lands him in Paris during the German occupation and he is, to say the least, a character who lacks conviction and interest. Nevertheless, despite its literary flaws, *All Men Are Mortal* maintains de Beauvoir's plea for commitment. People can never be free as individuals, the novel argues, until they are prepared to fight for the rights of others.

But that position, as de Beauvoir quite clearly perceived, was full of difficulties, not the least of which is the problem that in fighting for the freedom of others, we may threaten or destroy the lives of those people whose freedom we are concerned to safeguard. *The Blood Of Others*, de Beauvoir's 'Resistance' novel, tackles the issue which she describes in *The Prime of Life* as having tormented her and Sartre during the war: the issue of German reprisals after acts of sabotage by the Resistance. Neither de Beauvoir nor Sartre was in any position to take up arms against the Germans, but they clearly perceived the dilemmas of those who did, and who in doing so brought about the death of innocent civilians. As the Germans rounded up and shot random members of the community every time the Resistance killed a German or damaged any installation essential to German military needs, the moral dilemma of all those involved – at whatever distance – in the Resistance was clear. This question, faced time and time again by French Resistance workers during the war, constitutes the background to *The Blood of Others*, in which the issue of moral responsibility is discussed in both abstract and particular terms. We are, however, told de Beauvoir's view on the matter before we read the novel, since it is prefaced with a quotation from Dostoevsky, 'Each man is responsible for everything before everyone.' The implication of this remark is clear: we have responsibilities to other specific individuals, but over and above these are other responsibilities, crucially to the values of freedom and liberty. Unless we are prepared to fight for those general values, our particular commitments are nonsensical, since we are turning our backs on the creation and maintenance of those conditions in which the freedom of individuals can be realized.

The Blood of Others concerns one man, Jean Blomart, who has chosen to take part in the Resistance, but is faced, at the beginning of the novel, with the dilemma of whether or not he should continue in its activities. As the novel opens, Blomart is seated at the bedside of his lover, Hélène Bertrand, fatally injured in a mission against the Germans. There is no doubt that Hélène will die, and her death is to Blomart both a cruel personal blow and an occasion on which to review his attitude to his fight against the Germans. As he well knows, every time he attacks the Germans he risks his own safety, and the safety of those working with him and of those unknown others who might be shot in reprisal. He has made his own decision about the risks he wishes to run with his own life, but Hélène's death brings home to him the anguish that his actions may well cause others. He has no reason to suppose that Hélène regrets her part in the Resistance, but as Blomart knows, all those others involved in the consequences of his actions have not made the same choices as himself. Convention, culture, and his own emotional inclinations all suggest to him that there should be no more deaths like that of Hélène: Blomart cannot but feel that he has caused her death. But rational thought, and political and ethical choice, all persuade him to another decision, that of continuing with his part in the Resistance. Despite the persuasive arguments in the novel against such action, the most telling of which is a remark by Blomart himself that 'it is easy to pay with the blood of others', he decides that freedom for all can only be guaranteed by decisions and confrontations which sometimes jeopardize individual freedom and life.

De Beauvoir's own personal commitment to freedom is an unquestionable hidden element of all the three existentialist novels. Although by no means didactic, the novels are not ambiguous in their conclusions: freedom has to be fought for, even if the means of those struggles involve pain and sacrifice. The death of Hélène in *The Blood of Others* is less troublesome in this respect than the murder by Françoise of Xavière at the conclusion of *She Came to Stay*. Françoise undoubtedly assumes that killing Xavière is the only way of maintaining her relationship with Pierre, and she uses her freedom of action to preserve what she values most in the world. However guilty Xavière is – and by the end of the novel there cannot be much doubt in the minds of most readers that she is a scheming and manipulative young woman – it is the ultimate denial of her freedom to murder her. And yet the novel suggests that we are wrong to leap to this conclusion; is there not a case for supposing that Xavière, in her wilful and knowing attempts to wreck the relationship of Pierre and Françoise and make both unhappy, is a deserving victim? By her own actions, Xavière has made an enemy of two people who (particularly Pierre) have only ever shown her kindness and consideration. She has, therefore, created conditions in which it might be argued that her murder is entirely justifiable. By betraying the liberty and freedom which she possesses, and by seeking to oppress and manipulate others, Xavière has brought upon herself her own destruction. That this destruction takes a particularly final form does not alarm de Beauvoir. Death is not, to her, an event which is tragic even if it comes before the general entitlement of three score years and ten. Since she rejects the bourgeois notion of life-as-a-career, she sees every day and every part of human existence as complete and important. Life is not cumulative, and there is therefore no reason to mourn death if it comes before its appointed time. Indeed, de Beauvoir was to write in 1946 that she saw no reason to oppose the death penalty. She argued that since some people deliberately set out to damage the freedom and liberty of others, there is little point in confronting those individuals with anything except retribution in the fullest possible sense: 'when a man deliberately and relentlessly degrades other men by turning them into objects, it is a public offence for which nothing can make amends?'[4] Thus Françoise does not emerge from *She Came to Stay* as the jealous murderer, the betrayed and injured mistress, which conventional interpretations might make her. She is deeply conventional in that she directs her anger against the female intruder into her life with Pierre, rather than against the faithless Pierre, but like Hélène in *The Blood of Others* she is not easily tagged with the label of innocent victim.[5] Both women chose their fate, realized the consequences of their actions, and in the fullest existentialist sense, lived. They demonstrate very fully the kind of human being and the form of morality which de Beauvoir admires. But the shortcomings of this morality deserve some attention.

The criticisms that can be levelled against de Beauvoir's moral system apply throughout her work. First, she pays almost no attention to the material circumstances which curtail the exercise, not to mention the conceptualization, of freedom. All individuals are thus in perfect, equal control of their destinies. This assumption leads to a second problem in de Beauvoir's work, and a crucial one from the point of view of feminism: her failure to distinguish between moral values and constraints imposed upon, and internalized by, men and women. That is not to say that de Beauvoir does not recognize the subordination of women; the acknowledgement of women's subordinate state is a constant premise of her work. But what is not suggested is the possibility that women's moral values are not less developed than those of men, but different. The point has recently been forcefully made by Carol Gilligan in *In a Different Voice*: women are far from being the morally inadequate or childlike creatures that is sometimes supposed, but they conduct their lives according to different principles (Gilligan 1983). What de Beauvoir fully realizes is that women are constantly being asked to adopt men's perceptions and values. What she arguably does not do is assert the validity of female behaviour and values. The existence of different concepts of morality between the sexes is not, therefore, raised by de Beauvoir as a problem.

To a considerable degree this deficiency arises from de Beauvoir's perception of all human beings as potentially equally able to realize their own freedom. Indeed, the elevation of that value above all others tends towards a political and social analysis that is potentially as much part of the ideology of the political right as of the political left. Although de Beauvoir makes plain throughout her life her abhorrence of bourgeois society, its pieties, and its hypocritical morality, this does not in itself place her on the political left. As Anne Whitmarsh has pointed out in her thorough examination of de Beauvoir's politics, de Beauvoir only discussed politics in ethical terms, giving particular attention to the issue of freedom. Whitmarsh writes:

'When she considers freedom in the political context, one of her major quarrels with Marxism comes to the fore. In her view, if you are fighting for socialism you are fighting for freedom, and when threats to freedom come from within Marxism they are unacceptable. As an existentialist, she believes that man is free to accept or reject the situation in which he finds himself, therefore she cannot accept historical determinism. Thus the disappearance of the proletariat as a class, which is imperative, is so in moral terms only, not because it is dictated as an inevitable historical process; it depends on those who are oppressed realising this and doing something about it. They are free to submit or revolt: their future cannot be imposed from outside by, for instance, the Communist Party.'

(Whitmarsh 1981: 63)

In an analysis of the class struggle, the assumption that the proletariat has only to realize its lack of 'freedom' in order to bring about a socialist society is more than inadequate; it suggests an almost complete ignorance of the realities of social existence of the majority of any population in any country. But inevitably, a conceptualization of oppression in terms of something described as 'freedom' lends itself to lack of interest in the conditions of material life. De Beauvoir obviously has real sympathy for the poor and the materially oppressed, but there is very little indication in either her autobiography or her other work of an understanding that some people simply have no choice about the nature of their existence.

Material issues and problems are not totally absent from de Beauvoir's work, but they are completely invisible in the sense that they are not understood to have any effect on the nature or the extent of human actions. She urges women to construct their own fate for themselves, but has little to offer in the form of advice about how a woman brought up in conditions of oppression can go about doing this. What is occasionally suggested in *The Second Sex* is a state in which women will wake up in the morning, decide to be 'free', and then go about constructing the conditions of freedom. The ties between human beings, those complex interactions which are often both supportive and oppressive, and, perhaps above all, the weakness of the material situation of most women are all factors which play little part in her analysis of either the actions of individuals or the structure and processes of the social world.

But this is perhaps inevitable, since de Beauvoir explicitly rejects in *The Prime of Life* both Marxism and psychoanalysis, the two major accounts of social organization and human motivation which might have led her to reconsider her view that human beings have only to want their freedom in order to be able to realize it. Both Marxism and psychoanalysis are seen by de Beauvoir as over-deterministic, and it is apparent from *The Prime of Life* and *The Second Sex* that de Beauvoir's knowledge of both Freud and Marx was limited. She and Sartre did not therefore follow the path of others of their generation towards either Marxism or psychoanalysis; both of them regarded Freud and Marx as guilty of excluding from their interpretations of the social and psychological worlds any space for self-determination. In 1952, in *The Communists and the Peace*, Sartre summed up his attitude to the question of the extent to which people create the conditions of their existence by saying 'Man is only what he makes of himself'. Subsequently modified, this view succinctly expresses the essential position of de Beauvoir throughout the majority of her work. Given this conceptualization of the individual in the social world it is hardly surprising that what emerges from de Beauvoir's work is a view of human beings as creatures who barely interact at all in any dialectical sense with their environment: they only swallow it or spit it out. What is not allowed is that even the most active opponent of bourgeois society, a person diametrically opposed to all the structures and processes of that society, might possess within his or her personality and emotional structure residual elements of bourgeois culture.

By far the best example of a human being committed to rational self-determination but containing such residual values and emotions is de Beauvoir herself, and nowhere is this more clear than in her short work about the death of her mother, *A Very Easy Death*. De Beauvoir and her mother had existed in a state of mutual tolerance for decades; de Beauvoir's rejection of Catholicism had deeply upset her mother, but there had never been a formal breach between mother and daughter and as both lived in Paris they had maintained a reasonably close, if not particularly intimate, relationship. In 1963 de Beauvoir's mother had an accident: she fell and broke her femur. Admitted to hospital, Madame de Beauvoir was discovered to have cancer. After a series of operations, she died. This bald statement of fact obscures the awful suffering of the dying woman, the absurd medical procedures that were doomed to failure, and the occasionally callous and ridiculous attempts of the medical staff to give hope when none existed. As an indictment of the way in which modern medicine can inflict enormous pain and hardship on patients, *A Very Easy Death* is a most powerful work. De Beauvoir describes most succinctly and economically the way in which doctors are often ill-equipped to cope with fatal illness: their training, geared towards the curing of disease, apparently cannot cope with those situations in which is is unlikely that the patient will live. The open admission of impending death, of a disease which was incurable, was a possibility which Madame de Beauvoir's doctors, like many doctors elsewhere, could not admit.

But powerful as it is as a treatise on the problem of death in a medical system which increasingly regards itself as all-conquering, *A Very Easy Death* is more important in terms of the light which it sheds on de Beauvoir herself, and the effect on her of those emotional forces she had previously so confidently dismissed. In *A Very Easy Death* she acknowledges that her mother had often irritated and annoyed her. She wrote of one of their frequent meetings:

'I would knock. I would hear a little moaning noise, the scuffling of her slippers on the floor, another sigh; and I would promise

myself that this time I should find things to talk about, a common
ground of understanding. By the end of five minutes the game
was lost: we had so few shared interests! I leafed through her
books: we did not read the same ones. I made her talk; I listened to
her; I commented. But since she was my mother, her unpleasant
phrases irked me more than if they had come from any other
mouth. And I was as rigid as I had been at twenty when she tried
(with her usual clumsiness) to move on to an intimate plane. "I
know you don't think me intelligent; but still, you get your vitality
from me. The idea makes me happy." I should have been
delighted to agree that my vitality came from her; but the
beginning of her remark utterly chilled me. So we paralysed each
other. It was all that she meant, when she looked firmly at me and
said, "You frighten me, you do".'

(VED, 61)

But the fear was not, perhaps, one-sided. De Beauvoir had no need to
fear any attack or hostility from her mother, but what she might have
felt is the enormous emotional vulnerability that parents sometimes
create in their children on certain issues. In her fight to escape from her
parents' world de Beauvoir had had to make herself impervious to their
emotional claims, and to maintain, in the face of some considerable
odds, that her own world was entirely satisfactory. To admit
unhappiness in the life which she had created might well have exposed
de Beauvoir to those emotions from her parents, and particularly her
mother, which she most feared – emotions of pity, self-righteousness,
and, most threatening of all, an attempt to draw the errant daughter
back by the demonstration of affection which had failed or been lacking
elsewhere. The commonplace maxim that a 'mother's love never ends'
can be both a promise and a threat: a life-long commitment to the child
which a mother has borne but equally a life-long hold on the primary
emotional loyalty of that child.

In *The Second Sex* de Beauvoir analyses the complexities of
relationships between mothers and daughters, and stresses the
ambiguity of the attitude of mothers to their growing daughters. On the
one hand, mothers are delighted to see their children growing up, on
the other that very process contains the threat that the mother will
become redundant. The mother therefore watches her adolescent
daughter facing the promises and hopes of adult life with mixed
feelings. A feeling of pride in a daughter's achievements, or beauty, or
popularity, is coupled with envy at the prizes that the daughter might
achieve which have been denied to the mother. Inevitably, if a

daughter does not achieve any great success, or make a spectacular marriage, but merely reproduces her mother's life, sadness at an unfulfilled life might well be mixed with a relief that the daughter has not escaped the fate of the mother. Since de Beauvoir so publicly and so obviously did not reproduce her mother's life, but became famous, rich, and highly successful, this pattern was not to be found in their lives. But this can only have heightened her mother's confusion about her own life: what kind of mother can she have been to have produced a daughter whose sexual liaisons and political opinions made her a figure of international fame, if not notoriety?

From *A Very Easy Death* it is clear that Madame de Beauvoir never resolved her conflicting views about her daughter. Yet it is equally clear that her daughter has her own share of unresolved conflicts, not the least of which is the general, theoretical problem of how young children are to be wanted, loved, and cared for without the emasculation to both mother and child of the conventional processes of child care. In *The Second Sex* de Beauvoir quotes Hegel's dictum that 'the birth of children is the death of parents' with apparent approval, and she obviously endorses the idea that to bear a child, or to become the father of one, changes an individual's life in an entirely unrewarding way. But at the same time as she highlights the dangers of maternity (and to a lesser extent paternity) her own experience demonstrates the rewards to a child of that care which demands total commitment from the mother. In *Memoirs of a Dutiful Daughter* she tells us of her mother's continuing and conscientious care for herself and her sister, and admits that this dutiful mothering was of fundamental importance in her development. She is therefore bound to her mother by those immensely effective ties of gratitude and obligation between children and parents, ties which frequently contain as much implicit hostility as explicit gratitude.

But de Beauvoir's analysis of emotional life, which suggests that all emotions are amenable to rational control, can only reject the problems raised by the ties between parents and children, or the particular forms that these ties take. Hence, de Beauvoir's method of explaining and coping with her mother is to analyse the social world which produced her mother and to place a great deal of blame for the unhappy and distorted relationship between her mother and herself on the social forms that dictated certain kinds of conventional parent–child and mother–daughter relationships. That analysis is entirely praiseworthy: people in all cultures do bear children whom they might not want, and children are brought up in ways which predictably produce conflict between them and their parents. In a post-Laingian and post-feminist world, these conflicts are well known and fully documented. But the question still remains of what kind of relationship should exist between parent and child. It is an issue which has a number of different ingredients. First, there is the issue of whether or not an instinct to bear and procreate children is a given, natural feature of human psychology. Second, there is the problem of how children should be brought up: the tonnage of books produced on the subject and the diversity of patterns suggest that no definitive answer exists. Only two consistent features emerge from the vast amount of literature on bearing and rearing children: for many human beings procreation is an essential part of sexuality, and the ties between parents and children transcend rational understanding.

That de Beauvoir felt both hostility and intense affection towards her mother is thus entirely comprehensible to her readers, if not to herself. *A Very Easy Death* bears witness to the intensity of the emotional links between parents and children: in the book de Beauvoir expresses the kind of grief at the death of her mother that she had never shown before, even when confronted by the death of people much closer to her, in intellectual and political terms, than her mother had ever been. The death of her friend Zaza (Elizabeth Mabille) and that of the young student Bourla had deeply upset her, but the kind of desolate deprivation which she describes when her mother died is unparalleled. Even de Beauvoir's account of Sartre's death — in which both the final paragraph and the preface express, with absolute economy, absolute loss[6] – has not the same air of wild and desolate grief as her description of the death of her mother. What dies with her mother is more than a somewhat hostile parent: it is an assumption of absolute and unqualified love that can exist between parent and children but is unlikely to be found elsewhere. For a rationalist such as de Beauvoir, a very real part of her grief at her mother's death must have been the realization that what she was mourning was not rational: it was an irrational, unchosen association between two people who became, as the child grew older, virtual strangers to one another. To mourn the death of a parent is, for anyone, a complex process. The different features of relief at final freedom from a disliked adult, guilt at an imperfectly realized relationship, and regression to the world of childish emotional insecurity are all common, and are all to be found in *A Very Easy Death*.

But the overriding feature of *A Very Easy Death* is a sense of the author's amazement at the strength of the emotional ties between herself and her mother. At the end of the book de Beauvoir writes:

'Generally speaking I thought of her with no particular feeling. Yet in my sleep (although my father only made very rare and

insignificant appearances) she often played a most
important part: she blended with Sartre, and we were happy
together. And then the dream would turn into a nightmare: why
was I living with her once more? How had I come to be in her
power again? So our former relationship lived on in me in its
double aspect – a subjection that I loved and hated. It revived
with all its strength when Maman's accident, her illness and her
death shattered the routine that then governed our contacts.'

(VED, 89)

Rationally, then, the mother was a not particularly likeable mother. In
the unconscious, symbolic world, however, she was an immensely
significant and potent force: a person with real emotional power and
control. That this power is unchosen and unwelcome makes her mother
intensely problematic for de Beauvoir: symbolically the mother
represents all those forces, of exclusive love, jealousy, emotional need,
and emotional dependence, that she had attempted to exclude, or place
on a rational level, in her own life. The death of the representative of the
irrational confronted de Beauvoir with an immensely powerful
challenge to her carefully controlled rational understanding of the
world. In particular, it suggested that love is not merely about
rationally assessed and chosen commitment, it is also about human
fears of isolation and abandonment which have their roots in the state
of dependence that constitutes childhood. Escaping from those childish
fears demands the care of parents, yet at the same time residual fears of
loss and deprivation inevitably remain. These elements of the human
condition find scant sympathy in de Beauvoir's autobiographical work.
Only in her fiction, and in *A Very Easy Death*, do we find the possibility
that emotional life is about more than the rational decisions of adults
who are in complete control of their emotional destinies. Human
freedom, these works suggest, is neither as widely available nor as
unproblematic as de Beauvoir's non-fiction would suggest.

3
_____ *The Second Sex* _____

Although it is apparent from de Beauvoir's *A Very Easy Death* and her account of Sartre's last years and death (*La Cérémonie des adieux*) that in her own life she had by no means resolved the problems that are created by emotional ties and needs (whether of mother and daughter or man and woman) she is nevertheless often held up as a model of triumphant rationality. She is seen as a woman who has lived an independent life, asserted her autonomy, and offered to other women an analysis of how their situation, of dependence and subordination, might be changed. It is assumed that de Beauvoir's life has been free from male control and influence: although emotionally engaged with men, she has, it is thought, never been subject to them in terms either of day-to-day control or of the more diffuse intellectual and emotional control of a reliance and dependence on a male other.

But it is questionable whether de Beauvoir is as emancipated from male domination as is sometimes claimed, for there is much in both her personal and her intellectual life to suggest that however materially and socially liberated from male control she was, some of the values, sentiments, and aspirations expressed both for herself and for others in her work are derived from male expectations and assumptions about the organization of the material and emotional world. Her uncritical belief in what she describes as rationality, her negation and denial of various forms of female experience, and her tacit assumption that paid work and contraception are the two keys to the absolute freedom of womankind, all suggest a set of values that place a major importance on living like a childless, rather singular, employed man. Indeed, a reading of *A Very Easy Death* and de Beauvoir's novels could lead to the conclusion that de Beauvoir's message to her readers is dominated by her view that to live like a traditional woman is to invite unhappiness – far better to live like a traditional man. That is not to say that paid work, contraception, intellectual training, and emancipation from passivity and superstition are in themselves to be condemned but it is to suggest that de Beauvoir's account of women's experiences and the nature of sexual difference is sometimes too rigidly dichotomized between two sets of expectations about male and female behaviour. Moreover, the dichotomy is hierarchical in that it tends to assume that traditionally male activities (the exercise of rationality, independent action, and so on) are in some sense superior, and are instances almost of a higher form of civilization than those concerns – such as child care and the maintenance of daily life – that have traditionally been the preserve of women. Equally, the dichotomy negates the similarities between male and female emotional and intellectual needs and the many complex distortions and contradictions that result from the denial of – for example – a capacity for nurturing in men and for rationality in women.

But these qualifications about de Beauvoir's writing on women, and in particular *The Second Sex*, should not be allowed to diminish or obscure the fact that de Beauvoir's life and work remain major achievements in the history of women's emancipation from the confines of the household and domestic toil. From its first publication, *The Second Sex* has been a major landmark in discussions of relations between the sexes. Whether we agree or disagree with the conclusions of the book its significance lies in de Beauvoir's success in placing on the intellectual agenda three crucial questions about the nature of relations between the sexes, namely, the problem of the origin of sexual difference, the nature and the elaboration of sexual inequality and difference, and the issue of how men and woman should live. These issues still dominate feminist discussion, and form an important part of debates in a number of academic disciplines and in psychoanalysis. It is interesting to note in passing that *The Second Sex* includes little material from either of these sources: the work of Freud and his successors is given very short shrift, and the material – albeit limited – that had been accumulated by 1949 in the social sciences on sexual difference is largely ignored. The emphasis of the book is not, therefore, on work by others besides de Beauvoir who have been interested in the question of sexual difference but rather on those writers whose work (which is predominantly literary in form) reflects in one way or another prevailing attitudes about men and women.

Prior to the publication of *The Second Sex* in 1949 de Beauvoir wrote nothing explicitly about the condition of women, although the three novels which she had published by that date (*She Came to Stay*, *The Blood of Others*, and *All Men Are Mortal*) all contain strong, central female characters. In no sense, however, does this make de Beauvoir a feminist, nor is there anything specifically feminist about the way in which she presents the dilemmas which confront her female characters. From de Beauvoir's own account of her life and her intellectual and political development it is apparent that during her early adult life she never had any sense of being penalized or the victim of prejudice because she was a woman. Of her views on being a woman before writing *The Second Sex* she said:

> 'far from suffering from my femininity, I have, on the contrary, from the age of twenty on, accumulated the advantages of both sexes; after *She Came to Stay* those around me treated me both as a writer, their peer in the masculine world, and as a woman; this was particularly noticeable in America: at the parties I went to, the wives all got together and talked to each other while I talked to the men, who nevertheless behaved toward me with greater courtesy than they did toward the members of their own sex.'
>
> (FC, 189)

Many contemporary feminists might balk at some of the underlying assumptions of this passage, and suggest that what de Beauvoir is actually saying is that she has been very happy to reap all the privileges of success in a masculine world, while retaining the right to those small courtesies extended to women precisely because they are assumed to be an inferior sex. What de Beauvoir does not question is the way in which success has been constructed, the social practices through which those wives – whom she chose not to talk to, in favour of their husbands – probably provided the conditions that allowed their husbands to develop their talents, and be 'successful' in the commonly understood sense of the male professional world.

The fact that at least a large part of the female population is conditioned to regard it as appropriate for male success to be pursued at the cost of female interests is not suggested in the passage quoted above, nor, indeed in any of de Beauvoir's other remarks about her situation at the time of the genesis of *The Second Sex*. Throughout the volumes of her autobiography she always acknowledges the help and support which she received from Sartre. Indeed, it must be apparent to any reader of this account of de Beauvoir's life and work that it is impossible to write about de Beauvoir without also writing about Sartre, so close was the co-operation and communication between them. It was, in fact, Sartre who – by de Beauvoir's account – suggested that she should write a study of women: if de Beauvoir is the mother of contemporary feminism, then Sartre played the typically male role, analogous to the physical father of a child developed and nurtured by the attention of a woman.

But de Beauvoir could nurture and develop *The Second Sex* precisely because she did not share the responsibility of the majority of women. Childless and unmarried, de Beauvoir lived a life that was free from domestic concerns and commitments, and in *The Prime of Life* she acknowledged her limited familiarity with the world of women whom she describes as 'living normal married lives'. She writes:

'there was another advantage which I derived from these new
acquaintanceships. I knew very few women of my own age and
none who led normal married lives. The problems that
confronted people like Stépha, Camille, Louise Perron, Colette
Audry or me were, as I saw them, individual rather than generic.
I began to realise how much I had gone wrong before the war, on
so many points, by sticking to abstractions. I now knew that it *did*
make a very great difference whether one was Jew or Aryan; but it
had not yet dawned on me that such a thing as a specifically
feminine "condition" existed. Now, suddenly, I met a large
number of women over forty who, in differing circumstances and
with various degrees of success, had all undergone one identical
experience: they had lived as "dependent persons". Because I
was a writer, and in a situation very different from theirs – also,
I think, because I was a good listener – they told me a great deal; I
began to take stock of the difficulties, deceptive advantages,
traps, and manifold obstacles that most women encounter on
their path. I also felt how much they were both diminished and
enriched by this experience. The problem did not concern me
directly, and as yet I attributed comparatively little importance
to it; but my interest had been aroused.'

(PL, 572)

So de Beauvoir's entry into feminism – or at any rate the arousal in her of something approaching a consciousness of the specificity of the

female condition – occurred in a cerebral way that becomes apparent in
the early pages of *The Second Sex*. Having experienced no disadvantages
or difficulties in her own life that she could relate to her own sex, and
having received a considerable amount of help and support from a man
in her chosen vocation, de Beauvoir's attitude to women suggests a lack
of engagement with and experience of the subjectivity of femininity – an
attitude that has occasionally led critics of her work to see her as an
anti-feminist and/or misogynist.[1] These charges, in the light of de
Beauvoir's considerable public efforts to ameliorate the condition of
women, cannot, *in toto*, be substantiated. Even so, throughout *The Second
Sex* and her subsequent novels, it is sometimes difficult to gauge the
precise extent of de Beauvoir's sympathy with women.

Thus *The Second Sex* opens with what almost amounts to a complete
dismissal of the subject of women and femininity. A defensive tone is
immediately apparent, and de Beauvoir writes as one who has to justify
an interest in the condition of women:

> 'For a a long time I have hesitated to write a book about women.
> The subject is irritating, especially to women; and it is not new.
> Enough ink has been spilled in the quarrelling over feminism,
> now practically over, and perhaps we should say no more about
> it.'
>
> (SS, xiii)[2]

It is important to recall that these words were written not in the 1980s, but
in 1949, when the amount of ink spilt on feminism amounted to little
more than a trickle, and the existence of a feminist movement of any
great influence or significance was, at least in France, decades away.
There had been a struggle for women's suffrage in France in the 1920s
and 1930s but compared to Britain or the United States there was little
that amounted to a tradition of feminist thought or debate. It is thus
extraordinary that the book should open on this note – particularly as
the remainder of the introduction documents precisely why the condition of women needs examination and alteration. As de Beauvoir
points out, woman has always been man's dependant and has 'gained
only what men have been willing to grant; they have taken nothing,
they have only received' (SS, xix). This telling sentence, implying so
vividly and clearly the passivity of the female condition, with all its
endless attempts to win male favour, does not suggest to contemporary
readers a writer prepared to dismiss feminism as a dying cause. Hence
de Beauvoir introduces an element of anger, of the need for change, into
what appeared at first as if it might be a scholarly treatise into some
curious quirk of social organization. And a few sentences later in the
same section de Beauvoir states her unequivocal thesis:

'Women lack concrete means for organising themselves into a unit which can stand face to face with the correlative unit. They have no past, no history, no religion of their own; and they have no such solidarity of work and interest as that of the proletariat. . . . The bond that units her to her oppressors is not comparable to any other. The division of the sexes is a biological fact, not an event in human history. Male and female stand oppressed within a primordial *Mitsein*, and woman has not broken it. The couple is a fundamental unity with its two halves riveted together, and the cleavage of society along the line of sex is impossible. Here is to be found the basic trait of woman: she is the Other in a totality of which the two components are necessary to one another.'

(SS, 19)

Here, then, stand man and woman, and here too is revealed de Beauvoir's conception of the nature of the relations between men and women, one which derives directly from existentialism. The concept of 'the other' that is central to existentialism is equally central to *The Second Sex*. Indeed, the idea of woman as 'the other' is the central organizing thesis of *The Second Sex* and gives to the book – and to de Beauvoir's discussion of relations between men and women – a particular originality.

In conceiving of woman as 'the other' de Beauvoir follows the Sartrean notions of 'Lookers' and 'Looked-at' – those who are, in any situation, active, and others who are passive. But she also extends this formulation to include Sartre's concept of bad faith: if men are active and women are passive it is because women accept their subordination and objectification since this state offers to them certain privileges and advantages, not the least of which is the evasion of full, adult, moral responsibility. Or, as de Beauvoir puts it:

'To decline to be the Other, to refuse to be a party to the deal – this would be for women to renounce all the advantages conferred on them by their alliance with the superior caste. Man-the-sovereign will provide woman-the-liege with material production and will undertake the moral justification of her existence.'

(SS, xx)

But given that this is the case – that women reject the possibility of choice and moral freedom – then de Beauvoir's subsequent discussion (that is, Part One of *The Second Sex* which is entitled 'The Data of Biology') offers little hope for escape from this impasse, since de Beauvoir, in turning (apparently at Sartre's suggestion) to an examination of the biological differences between the sexes, adopts something of an essentialist view of biology. Of course, for many contemporary feminists the major premise of *The Second Sex*, namely de Beauvoir's assertion that women do accept their own objectification and deny their individual authenticity, is in itself deeply suspect since it implicitly denies those many situations in which women have asserted specifically female interests and identities, and refused that passive role, in relation to men and the constructed moral universe, which de Beauvoir assigns to them.

Yet given de Beauvoir's account of male and female biology, women's passivity is a natural given. In beginning *The Second Sex* with a discussion of biological sex differences de Beauvoir follows a quite orthodox path; many participants – not the least Freud in his 'Some Consequences of the Anatomical Differences between the Sexes' – begin their explorations with biology. But as in the case of Freud, what is crucial is what is made of biology: the differences between the reproductive systems of men and women and their external genitalia are in little dispute. Unlike Freud, however, de Beauvoir is more concerned with unseen physical data than with immediately obvious physiological differences. And she writes:

> 'the fundamental difference between male and female mammals lies in this: the sperm, through which the life of the male is transcended in another, at the same instant becomes a stranger to him and separate from his body; so that the male recovers his individuality at the moment when he transcends it. The egg, on the contrary, begins to separate from the female body when, fully matured, it emerges from the follicle and falls into the oviduct; but if fertilised by a gamete from outside, it becomes attached again through implementation in the uterus. First violated, the female is then alienated – she becomes, in part, another than herself. She carries the foetus inside her abdomen until it reaches a stage of development that varies according to the species – the guinea-pig is born almost adult, the kangaroo still almost an embryo. Tenanted by another, who battens upon her substance throughout her pregnancy, the female is at once herself and other than herself; and after the birth she feeds the new born upon the milk of her breasts.'

(SS, 19)

The metaphysical implications of this situation are clear: women, in the very acts of heterosexual intercourse and child bearing, are doomed by their biology to passivity and alienation.

De Beauvoir's account of biology – which includes a discussion of both human and animal life – is striking for the tacit assumptions that are made about the physical differences between men and women. It is doubtful if today many people (let alone many feminists) would be content to assume that the carrying and birth of a child is necessarily and essentially a passive act in the sense that de Beauvoir suggests. Women may be the carriers of unborn children but the acts of birth and lactation would be interpreted as involving more active participation on the part of the mother than de Beauvoir allows. Indeed, to a certain tradition in contemporary feminism, motherhood – in all its physical manifestations – is regarded as fundamentally active, and normal, while any attempt to detract from these qualities is seen as a feature of the patriarchal debasement of women's activities.[3] But apart from this issue (which is closely related to the constant problem throughout de Beauvoir's work of the extent to which she has so internalized patriarchal ideology as to fail to see alternatives to this perception), two other difficulties exist in de Beauvoir's account of sexual difference. The first is the way in which in the chapter on biology she progresses, in the most orthodox Darwinian way, from a study of the simplest organisms to those of the most complex – namely mammals. As Rosalind Coward has recently pointed out, Darwin's account of human reproduction and sexual differences assumes extensive general differences between men and women, and he is unwilling, she suggests, to investigate fully the extent of sexual similarity (Coward 1983: 76–80). Clearly, genital differences between men and woman exist but Darwin was among the first to perceive that it is perhaps too disruptive of our fundamental social categorization to ask too many questions about the extent of other differences between the sexes. De Beauvoir, in following Darwinian evolutionary theory, implicitly accepts the concept of general and extensive difference between male and female, man and woman, which now seems at least questionable.

A second underlying problem of de Beauvoir's discussion of sexual difference in human beings is her taken-for-granted belief that it is possible to make generalizations about human beings from a study of animal behaviour – a view repeated uncritically in her later work. Thus in the first chapter of *The Second Sex* de Beauvoir's account of animal life is often interchangeable with her descriptions of human society. For example, she writes of male mammals that:

> '(they) display almost no paternal instinct. Very often he
> abandons the female after copulation. . . . He is in general larger
> than the female, stronger, swifter, more adventurous; he leads a
> more independent life, his activities are more spontaneous; he is

more masterful, more imperious. In mammalian societies it is
always he who commands.'

(SS, 21)

Now as a general observation on the family life of mammals, and the
general characteristics of male mammals, the above may be perfectly
true. But the implication of this account can only be that the author
assumes some general state of 'male-ness' that transcends the other
differences that separate men from male apes and tigers. Indeed, this
impression is heightened by the way in which de Beauvoir scatters her
discussion of the differences between men and women (or male and
female animals) with quotations from Hegel and Heidegger on the
relative attributes of male and female. Since, according to these writers,
men (and the male) always emerge as active while women (and the
female) are inevitably passive, we can only assume that de Beauvoir is
prepared to overlook those other characteristics that separate people
from animal life, and accept a dichotomy that opposes all males to all
females.

Thus when de Beauvoir does turn to discuss human biology it is no
surprise that men and women appear as very different creatures. The
most striking difference between them – according to de Beauvoir – is
the degree of complication in the physical characteristics of men and
women. Men are awarded a brief nine lines to describe their progress
towards maturity. After puberty, 'the male sex life is normally
integrated with his individual existence: in desire and in coition his
transcendence towards the species is at one with his subjectivity – he *is*
his body' (SS, 23). Men are clearly fortunate, compared with women:
no problems of the body confront them between adolescence and the
grave. But as de Beauvoir darkly observes, 'Woman's story is much
more complex.' And not merely complex, but also crisis-ridden: 'from
puberty to menopause woman is the theatre of a play that unfolds within
her and in which she is not personally concerned', writes de Beauvoir,
viewing the functions of female biology with what can only be described
as a certain amount of distaste. And it is a distaste coloured by the view
that women's biology makes her inferior to man. In a passage on the
way in which men and women absorb calcium into their bodies de
Beauvoir writes:

'Instability is strikingly characteristic of woman's organisation in
general; among other things, man shows greater stability in the
metabolism of calcium, woman fixing much less of this material
and losing a good deal during menstruation and pregnancy. It
would seem that in regard to calcium the ovaries exert a catabolic

action, with resulting instability that brings on difficulties in the ovaries and in the thyroid, which is more developed in woman than in man. Irregularities in the endocrine secretions react on the sympathetic nervous system, and nervous and muscular control is uncertain. This lack in stability and control underlies woman's emotionalism, which is bound up with circulatory fluctuations – palpitation of the heart, blushing, and so forth – and on this account women are subject to such displays of agitation as tears, hysterical laughter, and nervous crises.'

(SS, 28)

Present-day readers may find it almost impossible to believe that this passage was written by a feminist, let alone someone who had just lived through a war in which the manifest psychological disturbances of many men had been demonstrated. But in de Beauvoir's defence it must also be said that she was writing in a generation in which some of the 'facts' of human physiology were not fully understood and at a time when such morally problematic areas of sexual relations as contraception, abortion, and homosexuality were not thought fit for discussion in polite society. For example, until the mid-1950s accurate information about the physiology of conception did not exist, and wholly intelligent and well-educated women thought it necessary to spend the first day of their menstrual period lying down.[4] So it is fully to de Beauvoir's credit that she raises the issue of human biology, even if in doing so she herself reflects many contemporary attitudes and misconceptions about women's biology, and too rapidly assumes that male biology is some sort of norm, from which women deviate. Indeed, a considerable amount of recent feminist polemic has been concerned to demonstrate that women's biology is only problematic to men, and in male terms. The argument has then been developed into the view that menstruation and pregnancy are physical attributes with positive features – a case totally different from de Beauvoir's in which these aspects of female biology are only ever conceived of in negative terms.

In her conclusion to the section on biology de Beauvoir writes that 'the body of woman is one of the essential elements in her situation in the world'. Yet to many readers the questions of how and why still remain. As already suggested, part of the problem of de Beauvoir's answer lies in her dichotomous conception of male and female biology. Equally, she can be seen to have accepted certain assumptions about the implications of male and female physiology. But some of these assumptions arise from de Beauvoir's essentially static conception of biology. This does not mean that people can alter the basic characteristics of their sexual identity, but that the part that these characteristics play in the determination of the conditions of human existence is very much a movable feast. Nothing will alter the fact that, for example, the reproductive systems of men and woman differ, but what will differ enormously between cultures and historical epochs is the extent to which biology affects the nature of an individual's life. In societies where contraception is unknown and the conditions of childbirth primitive it is obvious that biology will have not only a different, but also a greater impact on women's lives than in, say, a developed western society. It is also necessary to stress, as de Beauvoir does not, that sexual relations in general are matters not merely of battle between two opposing (if ill-matched) groups of individuals with different biological characteristics, but of often complex negotiations between individuals. We do not, therefore, have to abandon the view that there are general differences in social power between men and women to allow that in individual cases relations between the sexes do not follow a pattern of absolute, one-sided oppression and domination.

Given the dichotomy that de Beauvoir has established between men and women in her discussion of biology it is scarcely surprising that when she turns to Freud ('The Psyco-Analytic Point of View') and Engels ('The View of Historical Materialism') she tends to emphasize what each has to say about women specifically, rather than about relations between the sexes in general. Since she is also concerned to develop her argument about woman as 'the other' it is equally unsurprising that what is omitted from the work of Freud and Engels are those areas of their work which are concerned with similarities between the sexes: bisexuality in Freud disappears, as does the sense, in Engels' *The Origin of the Family, Private Property and the State*, that there is a community of interest between male and female bourgeois and proletarian. Indeed, de Beauvoir, in the case of Freud, makes a categorical assumption ('Freud never showed much concern with the destiny of women; it is clear that he simply adapted his account from that of the destiny of man, with slight modifications' (SS, 34)), that is, as subsequent writers have pointed out, quite simply inaccurate.[5]

So Freud is given little credence by de Beauvoir: she acknowledges the intellectual scope and range of his work but what she cannot countenance in psychoanalysis is the denial of choice: 'All psychoanalysts systematically reject the idea of choice and correlated concept of value, and therein lies the intrinsic weakness of the system' (SS, 40). It is, she continues, her intention to place women in the realm of freedom, to 'place woman in a world of values and give her behaviour a dimension of liberty'. But this was precisely Freud's intention: to emancipate both sexes from the prison of their refusal to understand

and integrate into their behaviour their sexuality. De Beauvoir and
Freud thus share a great deal more than she allows – with the major
difference that her answer to the question of what to do about sexual
difference is largely to negate, if not deny it. Thus while Freud suggests
that women, and men, should accept their biology and understand the
powerful distortions in behaviour that result from its suppression, de
Beauvoir tends to argue that women should view with suspicion the
usual expressions of female sexuality: namely marriage and maternity.

Seen from the 1980s, the suspicion with which de Beauvoir views
maternity and marriage might seem to some to be occasionally
exaggerated. Yet in de Beauvoir's account of both there is much that
remains pertinent: her discussion of maternity rightly raises crucial
questions about the reasons for women's desire for children and the
complex of male/female relations in which a desire for a child becomes
paramount. Equally, de Beauvoir's suspicion of conventional heterosexual relationships remains valid in an age which has seen twenty
years of sexual libertarianism without any significant shift in the power
relations of men and women. Even so, curious contradictions remain a
puzzling part of *The Second Sex* and its part in feminist history: de
Beauvoir contributes towards the establishment of a feminist tradition
that is avowedly anti-Freud yet at the same time does not question the
'normality' of sexual desire being heterosexual (some passages in the
section on lesbianism contain crudely stereotypical portraits of
lesbians); she is rightly sceptical about a 'natural' female desire for
maternity and thus does not constitute part of the feminist cult of
motherhood; and last, but not least, a curious ambivalence about
female-ness and femininity runs throughout *The Second Sex*. De
Beauvoir's case against femininity as traditionally constructed (and
traditionally reflected in some of the more misogynist works of western
culture which she examines) is very powerful, yet what remains
problematic is the political implication of the book: women must assert
their independence from the state of 'otherness' assigned to them by
men and male culture, but if they do this, and if we agree with de
Beauvoir that what is feminine is what has been constructed in
dependence and subservience (and must therefore be rejected), we
must also ask where this leaves women.

Where de Beauvoir leaves women is as autonomous and independent beings: her new woman (described in the concluding chapters
of *The Second Sex*) is a free and active person:

> 'The emancipated woman wants to be active, a taker, and refuses
> the passivity man means to impose on her. The "modern"

woman accepts masculine values: she prides herself on thinking, taking action, working, creating on the same terms as man.'

(SS, 676)

Here is the free woman – doing, acting, and choosing on the same terms as men. But while this condition may sound attractive to some, to others it raises a host of problems about exactly what de Beauvoir is proposing. What does not seem to be included in her outline of the future is any change in men except in so far as changes are forced upon them by the new woman's greater inclination to argue and reject the more extreme instances of male control. So women of the new era have to carry what might almost be described as a double burden in that they have to relinquish the safety of the position of the dependent other, but it is not expected that the world of men into which they move will have radically altered. (For example, it is pertinent to ask about that 'original aspiration to dominate the other' which the human consciousness apparently possesses in this new order: is it to be assumed that it will disappear?) Certainly it is true that de Beauvoir expects that the new woman will provoke a new reaction in men and that more egalitarian sexual relationships will result from this change, but essentially the world of men, and their activities and values, seem to stay much the same. De Beauvoir does not advocate, like later feminists, the reorganization of the social world so that, for example, men take an equal share in child care, nor does she ask exactly what will constitute equality between the sexes. Her plan for the future is essentially reorganization of the education and socialization of girls: they are to be brought up to be active and intellectually competitive. Consequently:

'Authorised to test her powers in work and sports, competing actively with the boys, she would not find the absence of a penis – compensated by the promise of a child – enough to give rise to an inferiority complex; correlatively, the boy would not have a superiority complex if it were not instilled into him and if he looked up to women with as much respect as to men. The little girl would not seek sterile compensation in narcissism and dreaming, she would not take the fate for granted; she would be interested in what she was doing, she would throw herself without reserve into undertakings.'

(SS, 683–84)

Boys and girls would arrive at adolescence regarding each other as equals, the onset of menstruation would hold no fears for girls who had already been taught to be at home with their physical selves. The 'new' young girl thus emerges into adult life with no fears about her body and no sense of personal inferiority.

A belief in the ameliorative and redemptive power of education and/or educational reform remains to this day a central belief of liberals and liberal feminists. From Mary Wollstonecraft to Betty Friedan it has been argued that if only young girls were educated more rigorously, differently, more competitively, or just more, then many of the inequalities between the sexes would disappear. De Beauvoir's conclusion to *The Second Sex* places her firmly within this tradition. Despite the way in which the book is organized and structured (that, is the analytical framework of existentialism) the final conclusions are essentially liberal: educate women differently and female subordination will cease. And in so far as this case goes, its strength and its value are undeniable: much in the past and present education and socialization of girls has been negative and dismissive of their talents. So to restructure the nature of their education would be no mean service.

But having reorganized the education and socialization of girls and produced a generation that has been brought up under this new regime, the problem is surely that these people enter an old world: one in which the sexual division of labour between adults remains unaltered, class divisions remain intact, and hierarchical structures of social and political control are the norm rather than the exception of social organization. The generation of women that emerged from the colleges of North America in the 1950s had benefited from an extensive higher education, yet Betty Friedan was to find women in their hundreds locked into suburban misery and seeking fulfilment in maternity and voluntary work. Friedan's answer to this problem 'which has no name' was to advocate a different kind of education: teach women mathematics and science, she argued, and they will deal more coolly and rationally with the problems of the adult world.[6] Equally, in the 1970s and the 1980s, liberal feminists advocate the reorganization of the school curriculum, the abolition of coeducation, and policies of positive discrimination towards women in education. All these changes would be of value, since it is still manifestly apparent that girls throughout the west are not given the same education as boys either in terms of the specific content of the curriculum or in the more diffuse terms of encouragement and reward. Undoubtedly, change in these areas would contribute towards the goal of a more sexually egalitarian society.

But the crucial point is that these changes could only *contribute* towards this new world. The liberal solution of more, and different, education has at some point to confront the problem of the social structure of the world outside the classroom and the lecture hall. Generally, the class structure is the rock on which liberal education policies founder and are found wanting; in the case of de Beauvoir's politics and prescriptions it is both the class and the sex structure of the west which provide hazards to her hopes of change. The case about woman as 'the other' in *The Second Sex* is powerful, but two problems seriously weaken its long-term strength and usefulness. The first is the absence in the book of the social world, and the second is the nature of de Beauvoir's attitude to female biology and femininity that has already been suggested.

To say that the social world is absent from *The Second Sex* may at first suggest that the scores of pages which de Beauvoir devotes to a discussion of history, myth, and literature have been overlooked. On the contrary, nobody reading *The Second Sex* could fail to notice these extensive descriptions of the perception of women. But what is so extensively documented is ideology – women in novels, in plays, in diaries, and in myth. To take just one example which is not untypical of de Beauvoir's approach to the elaboration and justification of her argument: de Beauvoir is arguing that women seldom know the ties of strong friendship and support, and writes:

> 'Women's fellow feeling rarely rises to genuine friendship, however. Women feel their solidarity more spontaneously than men; but within this solidarity the transcendence of each does not go out toward the others, for they all face together toward the masculine world, whose values they wish to monopolize each for herself.'
>
> (SS, 513)

This questionable statement is then followed by an example to illustrate its truth – but the example comes not from data about the real world, but from Tolstoy's *War and Peace*. And the pattern is far from untypical; de Beauvoir proposes a thesis about women, or men's perception of them, and then proceeds to illustrate it by reference to literature. The substantiating footnote – to which every academic or scholarly reader always turns when doubtful about the veracity or origin of an argument – is largely absent from de Beauvoir. In a work of fiction or philosophy, such an absence would be of little note or absolute irrelevance, but *The Second Sex* claims to be an examination of the situation of women in the social world, and it is therefore not altogether unjustified to ask for some evidence of at least a cursory glance at its structures and processes.

Despite its considerable strengths as argument and polemic *The Second Sex* therefore contains a central problem in terms of its relevance to the situation of women – namely that the actual situation of women in the social world is only thinly illustrated. Nowhere is this more apparent than in de Beauvoir's discussion of Engels. In her analysis of literature and myth she offers numerous insights and perceptive asides, and of course establishes that tradition within feminism which was to provide the inspiration for the works of those members of a younger generation such as Kate Millett and Eva Figes who were concerned to show, *à la* de Beauvoir, the extensively patriarchal nature of western literature and mythology. Yet the shortcomings of these writers are also the shortcomings of de Beauvoir – they select authors to demonstrate their argument (D. H. Lawrence appears as a representative of misogyny in both Millett and de Beauvoir), and are often highly selective, as Cora Kaplan has so aptly pointed out in her critique of Millett, in the reading of texts (Kaplan 1979). So a discussion of Engels and *The Origin of the Family, Private Property and the State* should have provided de Beauvoir with an opportunity to correct the impression that she is solely concerned with the work of those who have elaborated and developed ideology rather than examined the structures and processes of the material world. Unfortunately, this is not what emerges from a reading of de Beauvoir on Engels, although it must immediately be said in her defence that in *All Said and Done* (the fourth volume of her autobiography, published in 1972) she remarked that if she was to rewrite *The Second Sex*, a major revision she would make would be to 'provide a materialistic, not an idealistic, theoretical foundation for the opposition between the Same and the Other' (ASD, 484). But in 1949 the material world, parti-cularly in the form of Engels and historical materialism, gets short shrift.

Engels appears in *The Second Sex* as the sole representative of historical materialism: Marx is barely mentioned and a scant ten pages are devoted to *The Origin of the Family*. (This scant attention has of course been corrected by later feminists who have now devoted a considerable amount of ink to Engels.) The reasons that de Beauvoir has little sympathy for Engels are twofold. First, she challenges Engels's assertion that the oppression of women is related to the ownership of private property. Second, she argues that the real reason for the oppression of women lies not in the organization of property relations but in the human desire to dominate, or as she describes it: 'If the human consciousness had not included the original category of the Other and an original aspiration to dominate the Other, the invention of the bronze tool could not have caused the oppression of women' (SS, 52).

Thus de Beauvoir, in rejecting Engels's account of the oppression of women, offers, implicitly, her own explanation: that there exists in the 'human consciousness' that desire to dominate that leads to the subordination of the powerless. So what is offered here is an essentialist view of human nature, in sharp contrast to the work of both Engels and Marx who were far more cautious about assuming that human beings had innate characteristics. Certainly, both Marx and Engels assumed that human beings had innate needs (to eat, sleep, and reproduce themselves) and that the capacity to work was an essential part of the human condition, but neither made categorical assertions about such possible psychological characteristics of human beings as the 'aspiration to dominate'.

But it is necessary to ask exactly who de Beauvoir is writing about when she tells us that 'human beings have a desire to dominate the Other'. She speaks of the 'human consciousness', but the sex that emerges as the dominated rather than the dominating is female. The question is thus immediately raised of whether it is just men who possess the characteristic of wishing to impose their will on others, while women languish in a state of passive acceptance. But even if they do, de Beauvoir's familiarity with the work of Hegel must lead us to suppose that she is familiar with the idea of master/slave relationships: a form of relation between human beings in which the apparently powerless and passive individual – simply by virtue of their powerlessness – controls far more within the relationship than is immediately apparent. Indeed, the remarks that de Beauvoir makes elsewhere (about, for example, the costs to women of giving up their subordination) suggest that she realizes only too well the potential emotional control over the other of the refusal of autonomy. What in fact this is then ascribing to women is a state of natural, almost innate, bad faith: men (the 'human beings') have a tendency to dominate, but women accept that domination. Engels, in his account of the 'world historic defeat of the female sex', did not suppose that the defeat took place for anything other than good material reasons – in this case the increasing importance of private property and women's divorce from its ownership and accumulation. Yet what de Beauvoir has done is to confuse material and psychological explanations: while she admits the existence of class, and class relations, the motivation of human beings (in this case the need to dominate others) is derived not from the relations of production but from innate characteristics.

An assumption that human beings have innate characteristics, coupled with the belief in the efficacy of education as a means of social change, places de Beauvoir – at least in so far as *The Second Sex* is concerned – clearly in the camp of those who subscribe to a view of human beings as less than perfect in the natural state, but capable of improvement. What is interesting about de Beauvoir, and her analysis of relations between men and women, is her highly selective view of what is natural and what is not. Most strikingly, and most originally, she excludes from her assumptions about what is 'natural' a desire on the part of women to bear children, of men to father them, and of men and women to form supportive and emotionally rewarding relationships between the sexes. Perhaps even more striking is the absence in *The Second Sex* of any suggestion of the ambiguities in rewards and values of relationships between men and women. Certainly, de Beauvoir portrays the frequent lack of openness and emotional honesty in human beings but what is missing is the rather more complicated possibility that relationships between individuals have a history, with different rewards and different costs for different parties at different points of time. But in a sense de Beauvoir paves the way for those feminists who see only constant exploitation in heterosexual relationships, a pattern unmitigated by changes in the life cycle, individual circumstances, or individual needs. It is hardly surprising that materialists among feminists have been on much firmer ground in their accounts of sexual relations: different wage rates for men and women, discrepancies in their access to social and political power can all be demonstrated by reference to evidence drawn from social reality.

Yet once feminists leave the areas of documented evidence and move into those areas – of literature and personal report – that largely form the basis for discussion in *The Second Sex* the ground becomes less firm: personal report is precisely that, and although literature can explore individual problems it is essentially individual in its subject matter. But if a writer is committed, like de Beauvoir, to an ethic of choice (and existentialism, according to her interpretation, is about nothing if not the centrality of choice in human actions), then there is little alternative except to explore issues of subordination and domination in personal terms, since all other terms undermine a belief in free choice by suggesting that human beings do not make absolutely free choices; indeed, Marx, Engels, and Freud, determinists one and all to de Beauvoir, were at pains to show that in contrast to the assumptions of optimistic liberals, people are everywhere bound by circumstances which are not of their making but within which they can make limited choices. So the rejection by de Beauvoir of Freud and Engels (and by implication Marx) points the way to those later feminists who, often for similar reasons, rejected their work. Freud has only recently been allowed a limited credibility in feminist circles; Marx has fared rather better, although it is striking that what is almost an aside in Marx, and a far from central thesis in *The Origin of the Family* (namely that only the entry of women into wage labour will ensure their emancipation), has received a disproportionate importance in the feminist condemnation of Marxism. Just as de Beauvoir condemns the Soviet Union for what she sees as its reactionary policies towards women, so some contemporary feminists have condemned Marxists, and Marxist feminists, for their assumption that class relations are of paramount importance, and that only a change in the social relations of production will emancipate women. Arguments such as that of Christine Delphy which attempt to demonstrate that gender divisions are of greater significance than those of class have not so far met with universal acceptance, even though many feminists have found – following de Beauvoir – that while it is relatively early to demonstrate similarities between women in ideological terms, a close examination of the social world reveals the limitations of this view.[7]

So in locating her argument about women very firmly in terms of an examination of ideology, de Beauvoir both grants herself leeway to choose her own material and excuses herself from that kind of close scrutiny which is generally directed against statements of fact. And as she says in *All Said and Done* she remains unrepentant about this choice: while the rewritten *The Second Sex* might have that greater materalist emphasis already mentioned she remains committed to the view that 'all male ideologies are directed at justifying the oppression of women, and that women are so conditioned by society that they consent to this oppression' (ASD, 484).

This is radical feminism with a vengeance: men are the natural oppressors of women, and women are so much the victims of patriarchal ideology that they have no defence against being colonized by its central principles. Women can only fight back by rejecting patriarchy – which to de Beauvoir means rejecting the passivity traditionally expected of women by men, and by becoming those independent beings who closely resemble the somewhat questionable male other. Yet if this is where de Beauvoir leaves women it is surely no surprise: the elements of her analysis of the situation of women (an essentialist view of male 'nature', a dichotomous conception of male and female, the powerful ingredient of the existentialist belief in the possibility of absolutely free choice, and the possibilities of a rational reappraisal of one's situation through the enlightened educational policies of others) all add up to a liberal, individualistic view of the world which can conceptualize natural dichotomies (in this case men or women, although it could equally well be black or white) but cannot encompass social differences that frequently restrict or eliminate choice. Thus when de Beauvoir calls on women, in the conclusion to *The Second Sex*, to emancipate themselves from femininity, the plea is for ideological emancipation, the call of the liberal for the 'new' attitude of mind, the 'new' politics, and a 'new' spirit. Certainly, assertiveness and a capacity to claim one's own rights are admirable features in any human being, but without a contextual discussion – of exactly why the claims are being made – the case is limited. Whatever the considerable strengths of *The Second Sex*, we must ask, therefore, if its call to arms inspired an army rather than pointed it towards any clearly defined target.

4
Women and men: the fiction

In *The Second Sex* de Beauvoir charts the excitement and nervous anticipation that adolescent girls entertain towards the possibility of entering social and sexual relations with men. The adolescent girl regards this possibility, according to de Beauvoir, with a mixture of excited anticipation and dread. On the one hand there lie the varied possibilities that men can offer to women and the wider social world that women, given male protection, can enter. On the other, negative, side is the cost of association with men – domestic tyranny and responsibility, pregnancy, the care of children, and a life of endless household drudgery.

The creatures who can both unlock the door of the world, and turn the key which shuts women out of it for ever, do not appear in *The Second Sex* as a particularly attractive group. Men possess what de Beauvoir describes as the 'original aspiration to dominate the Other', and, she argues, they have more than adequately demonstrated this proclivity in the past two thousand years of western history. Frequently careless and uncaring in their dealings with women, men emerge as insensitive and selfish creatures, content to brutalize women, and hypocritical in the moral systems which they erect to control women's behaviour. Men, as de Beauvoir points out, will frequently persuade or threaten women into adultery, abortion, moral compromise, and unprincipled action, yet are the same people who construct savage laws against divorce, or abortion, or women's economic independence. Relations between the sexes are therefore constructed around a dialectic of male dominance and female passivity, a form of relationship which encourages men in unthinking authoritarianism and dominance, and women in passivity and deviousness. Neither sex is free to express its true needs, each is constantly in danger of acting in bad faith towards the other. Yet the paradox of this analysis of existing relations between the sexes is that de Beauvoir seems to advocate the assumption by women of many male characteristics: as suggested at the end of the previous chapter, de Beauvoir wants women to escape from their subordinate and passive relationship to men by assuming precisely those habits and attitudes of rationality, independence, and emotional autonomy that have constituted the means by which men have been able to oppress women. Because men have generally been free of those ties to others which have traditionally been the lot of women, they have had both the time and the energy to develop intellectually, to explore the social world, and to organize the ideology of each and every society. If women are ever to imitate this activity, reasons de Beauvoir, they too must live independent lives and reject those relationships which constrain social action and mobility.

This prospect may seem to many to be less than appealing, particularly after almost two decades of western feminism have emphasized the values which women's traditional lives entail, values of nurturing, mutuality, care for others, and a morality which is less concerned with absolute, formal values than with the maximization of personal happiness and well-being. The activities of women in the household and particularly in child care are seen as positive; far from imprisoning women it is now suggested that these activities, and the values associated with them, are ones that men might well copy. The argument is not, therefore, that women should be more like men, but that men should be much more like women. The man who appears in *The Second Sex,* and indeed the traditional male of the west, is now seen as emotionally inexpressive, incapable of shared egalitarian relationships with others, and locked in futile competition and dreams of greatness and power. This 'macho' male, on feminist examination, looks quite unlike an enviable prototype of a human being. On the contrary, he appears as emotionally undeveloped, selfish, and, when given power, a real danger to the lives of others.

It is thus that a contemporary reading of *The Second Sex* might conclude that the very last thing that women should do to improve their

lot in life is to become more like men. Becoming the equal partners of
men in the kind of relationships which de Beauvoir outlines in the
conclusion to *The Second Sex* involves the taking on of many
characteristics of men, and almost certainly the abandonment of
maternity which remains a trap and a prison for women. Work (in the
sense of paid work outside the home) is the salvation of both sexes,
sexuality remains heterosexuality and yet becomes an unproblematic
meeting of two bodies of two different sexes. The disappearance of the
economic dependence of women on men is followed by the
disappearance of differing values, assumptions, and interests between
the sexes. It is not, perhaps, unreasonable to ask quite what women
have gained from this new, Utopian arrangement. Granted they have
been freed from rearing children, but what they have been liberated
into appears to be a world in which they may well be wage slaves rather
than house slaves, and be forced into the kind of emotional narrowness
that men have frequently been accused of illustrating, since their
emotional relationships are limited exclusively to sexual relationships
with other adults.

The elaboration and discussion of relations between the sexes is, of
course, a central theme of *The Second Sex*. Yet it is in her novels and short
stories that de Beauvoir most fully develops her views of male/female
relationships: in fiction she is able to show the history, and something of
the emotional complexities, of relationships between men and women
in a way that is impossible in *The Second Sex*, where individual instances
or relationships serve to illustrate a particular thesis. But it is clear that
de Beauvoir's novels are very much by the author of *The Second Sex*: in
both contexts a dichotomy is invoked between men and women, and in
both the only transcendence possible between the sexes is through
rational activity rather than emotional or sexual life. In the novels, just
as much as in *The Second Sex*, women have to 'escape' from the limits of
their biology; in fiction just as much as in fact there is no suggestion that
men might be asked to integrate women's biology into their understanding and the arrangements of the social world in such a way that women
are not trapped in a determining relationship with their anatomy.

If de Beauvoir's fiction is examined in its entirety, from the first
full-length novel to *The Woman Destroyed*, a general pattern can be
observed in which women stay much the same (in the sense that some
of the female characters appear over and over again in different novels
under different names) while the men become increasingly morally
unattractive and unsympathetic. Pierre, of *She Came to Stay*, is a
complex and morally sensitive man, while Maurice, of *The Woman
Destroyed*, is little more than a stereotypically selfish, adulterous

husband. And at the same time as the men become increasingly distant from moral concerns or emotional sensitivity, so the relationships between the sexes become more and more unhappy. The relationship between Françoise and Pierre in *She Came to Stay* (or Anne and Lewis in *The Mandarins*) are hardly romantic idylls, but they do contain an integrity and a concern for the other which is significantly absent in *The Woman Destroyed*. Since de Beauvoir's fiction spans a period in which women in western Europe achieved a measure of formal emancipation, and the sexual 'revolution' challenged accepted mores about sexuality, it is interesting that a perceptive and well-informed author sees these changes – and reflects these changes in her fiction – as losses rather than gains for women and portrays an overall worsening in male/female relationships.

Essentially, three stages exist in de Beauvoir's fiction: the first is that of the existentialist novels (*She Came to Stay*, *The Blood of Others*, and *All Men Are Mortal*), the second is that of the social novel (*The Mandarins*), and the third is that of what is perhaps best described as the stage of the novels of despair and moral anarchy: the collection of stories entitled *The Woman Destroyed* and the novel *Les Belles Images*. In these three stages of de Beauvoir's work we can detect quite different kinds of heterosexual relationships, and very varied pictures of men and women. In the first group of novels, de Beauvoir portrays heterosexual relationships as intensely passionate, sexually expressive, and above all collaborative: men and women are brought together by common interests and values. For example, in *She Came to Stay*, Françoise and Pierre, like Jean and Hélène of *The Blood of Others*, are united by common intellectual and political commitments, mutual agreement about how to live, and a shared moral code that operates between them and in their dealings with the rest of the world. De Beauvoir once wrote that she and Sartre had the 'same sign on their brows' and this description of the central relationship in her own life accurately summarizes the kind of relationship that exists between Françoise and Pierre, or Jean and Hélène. It is a pact against the world: an agreement between two people that they are united in the ways which they identify as absolutely central to their being.

But against these morally committed couples, de Beauvoir also poses the kind of couple which is to become, in *The Woman Destroyed*, a central theme. It is the couple in which the woman is totally emotionally dependent on the man, and is unable to achieve any kind of autonomous existence without reference to the relationship which she has with a particular man. The agonies for women of this kind of relationship are hinted at in all de Beauvoir's novels; thus Elizabeth, in

She Came to Stay, describes her feelings after she has seen a momentary touch of the hand between her lover Claude and another woman:

> 'for a moment or so, she stood motionless at the back of the auditorium. Claude was helping Suzanne to slip off her mink cape; then he sat down beside her; she leaned towards him and laid her hand on his arm. A sharp stabbing pain suddenly shot through Elizabeth. She recalled that December evening when she had walked through the streets drunk with joy and triumph because Claude had said to her: "You're the one I really love". . . . He loved her, but that had changed nothing.'
>
> (SCS, 73)

Elizabeth, like other female characters in de Beauvoir's later novels, suffers agonies of jealousy and misery because the loved one whom she still regards as central to her life is demonstrably no longer hers alone.

It is possible to find in the first stage of de Beauvoir's fiction all the problems in heterosexual relationships that she is to explore at greater length in her later work. But one further feature of all her novels, already apparent in her earliest work, deserves mention – de Beauvoir's assumptions about the nature and the extent of male and female sexuality. What emerges as a pattern in all the novels is that male sexual desire and expression are far less problematic than those of women. It is, moreover, men who show the greatest apparent inclination towards infidelity, or at least towards greater variety in their sexual partners than women. In *The Second Sex* de Beauvoir argued that male sexuality is far less beset with problems than that of women; thus in her novels she gives this statement of fact a fictional expression and repeatedly suggests a pattern of sexuality in which women invariably become deeply attached to the men with whom they have sexual relations, while the men are far more inclined to dismiss sexual encounters as unimportant, or at any rate place them at a far lower level of significance than do women. This pattern reflects the commonplace ideology of the west – that men have 'natural' sexual needs which have to be expressed (and have to be expressed with women) while women's sexual needs are far more generalized than those of men, and a great deal more emotionally charged. The 'ideology of male sexual needs' as Mary McIntosh has described it, is able to see fleeting male infidelities, female prostitution, or male sexual promiscuity as expressions not of major moral failing but simply as features of a world in which boys are expected to be boys (McIntosh 1978).

Few of de Beauvoir's male characters are, in fact, sexually promiscuous in any extravagant sense. Nevertheless, while not extending their sexual favours widely, they do inflict considerable emotional damage on their female partners by the encounters which they embark on. Some of these encounters are deeply charged and tortuous affairs, others are presented quite straightforwardly as indulgences of the flesh rather than the spirit. A shift occurs here between the first, existentialist, novels and *The Mandarins*: in the existential novels sexual relations are always seen as emotionally significant, while in *The Mandarins* passing sexual encounters are seen as precisely that, implying no commitment between the parties and certainly not indicative of any strong affection. Thus in *She Came to Stay* Pierre deliberates for some considerable time about embarking on a sexual relationship with Xavière while in *The Mandarins* two of the central (and sympathetically portrayed) characters – Anne and Henri Perron – apparently attach far less significance to their sexual encounters. A different attitude to sexuality is therefore apparent between the two stages of the fiction (and a gap of some seven years separates *The Mandarins* from *All Men Are Mortal*), and sexual relationships lose some of the emotional and social significance which had been a characteristic of the earlier fiction.

In *The Mandarins* it is noticeable that there is, in general, more diversity in the range of heterosexual relationships than in *She Came to Stay*, *All Men Are Mortal*, or *The Blood of Others*. While the archetypical relationship between men and women in these novels is that of the committed, sexually expressive couple, in *The Mandarins* something of a dichotomy emerges between relationships in which men and women share the same commitments (to political values or moral concerns), and yet are not sexually active partners, and those couples in which sexual passion and attraction is a major, if not the single, factor in the relationship. Thus in *The Mandarins*, these two kinds of relationships between men and women are represented by the relationship between Anne Dubreuilh and her husband Robert, and that between Anne and her American lover, Lewis Brogan. Side by side with the history of Anne's romance with Lewis, de Beauvoir portrays the end of the romance between Henri Perron and his mistress of ten years, Paula. The moral of the history of the relationship between Paula and Henri is quite clearly that, for women, to live for love is to die for love. When Anne turns her back on Lewis and the United States, and decides to return home to Robert and their somewhat austere life together, it is a decision that the reader cannot but endorse, given the terrible sufferings of Paula, a woman who abandoned everything for love. At the beginning of *The Mandarins* a brief conversation between Paula and Henri suggests the kind of stasis which their relationship has developed. The scene takes place just before a party, Paula appears dressed for the festivities in a violet dress:

> ' "You're so positively dedicated to violet!" he said smiling. "But you adore violet!" she said. He had been adoring violet for the past ten years; ten years was a long time. . . . It was all so useless, he told himself. In green or yellow he would never again see in her the woman who, that day ten years earlier, he had desired so much when he had nonchalantly held out her long violet gloves to her.'
>
> (TM, 12–13)

The emotional dependence of Paula on Henri traps them both into a deadly game: Henri cannot bring himself to tell Paula that he wishes to leave her, and contents himself with small, open infidelities (including, since this is a novel about intellectual life, a somewhat incestuous affair with the Dubreuilhs' daughter Nadine). Because Paula in a sense 'allows' Henri these affairs he becomes even more trapped; Paula gives him freedom, he cannot ask her for more, and so how is he to explain that what he wants is total disengagement? Eventually, their relationship ends, Paula becomes deeply involved in social life, and Henri is left with Nadine.

Against the unhappy relationship of Paula and Henri, de Beauvoir sets the relationship of Anne and Lewis Brogan. As de Beauvoir has acknowledged, the depiction of this affair is a fictionalized account of her own affair with the American novelist Nelson Algren – an account which Algren has condemned, both for its very existence and its content. Despite this controversial use of personal experience (and indeed the experiences of another party) in fiction, the affair is portrayed in essentially positive and romantic terms. But more surprising than the elements of either romance or commitment in the telling of the tale is the conventional nature of the sexuality and the sexual experience that occurs. Perhaps for some contemporary readers the most conventional aspect of the affair is that it is heterosexual; aside from that qualification it is also the case that the descriptions of the physical love of Anne and Lewis follow many of the conventions of romantic fiction. Thus de Beauvoir portrays the sexual encounters of Anne and Lewis in terms which suggest that female sexual drive is only brought to life by men. Rather like the heroines of the novels of Barbara Cartland or Denise Robins, Anne finds herself 'transformed' by male sexual desire. It is true that in the previous pages Anne had been preoccupied with wondering whether or not Lewis would initiate any sexual activity between them, but even if de Beauvoir does allow that

Anne might have had more than a passing interest in whether or not Lewis wanted to sleep with her, the moves towards this state are all for Lewis to make. Anne can desire, she can gaze longingly, but, as much of chapter six makes clear, it is Lewis who is expected to make the crucial, resolving gestures towards his bedroom. And once there, the transformation of Anne from disembodied self to a physically delighted human being occurs. Like lovers in romantic fiction, Lewis and, particularly, Anne sink into a rosy haze of delight.

But in de Beauvoir's work, as in romantic fiction, sexuality has to be organized in an appropriate, conventional, manner. This is the second surprising element of de Beauvoir's portrayal of sexuality, and is illustrated by the symbolic claiming by Lewis of Anne in a permanent relationship, expressed both through the expected 'language of love' in which the parties exchange, at appropriate moments, words of affection and commitment, and through his giving her a ring. After their night together, certain doubts seem to arise in Anne's mind, but 'There was no need to be upset; he was caressing my hair, speaking gently, simple words, slipping an old copper ring on my finger' (TM, 424). And again, only three pages later, when Anne is beset with doubts about the relationship Lewis is there with reassurance and the ring: 'At the lakeside, Lewis had spoken to me as if I were never going to leave him, and he had slipped a ring on my finger' (TM, 427). So love is 'organized' in the expected way, and the exclusivity and commitment which western culture expects in sexual relations between men and woman are reaffirmed. Yet what is surprising about this particular case (apart, of course, from the fact that some of the passages are astonishingly romantic for the author of *The Second Sex*) is that both Anne and Lewis fall so rapidly into conventional patterns in their affair, notably into the pattern that says that it is only possible for a human being to have one significant relationship with another person. Lewis is as jealous of Anne's life in Paris with Robert as Anne is of Lewis's ex-wife: they both have intense feelings towards the intimate friends of the other, and their relationship with each other moves rapidly towards the moment when Anne has to choose Lewis or Robert. De Beauvoir does not assume that Anne must love any man that she sleeps with (the encounter with Scriassine in chapter one is acknowledged as a compartmentalized affair of 'carnal pleasure') but what is to be found in *The Mandarins* (and elsewhere) is the assumption that love, passion, and mutual physical pleasure are the sources of feelings, and needs, of exclusivity and commitment. Whether or not this is actually the case about human emotional life is unknowable; all that can be asserted is that western culture values monogamy and yet allows compartmentalized, adulterous sexuality – the kind of sexual relations advocated by Sartre and de Beauvoir are deeply threatening to bourgeois society since they involve choice, and possibly the frequent change of sexual partners. As suggested in Chapter 1, de Beauvoir and Sartre faced in their own lives all the problems of people wishing to live outside conventional morality. The problems of their 'open' relationship were solved by Sartre through conventional deceit, and by de Beauvoir largely through abstaining from threatening relationships. Both advocated openness, honesty, and freedom in personal relations, but found (and de Beauvoir illustrated the problems in her fiction) that this blueprint was woefully inadequate for the emotional realities of relations with others. Human beings are capable of amazing intellectual feats, great rational understanding, and concern for others – but add sexuality into any relationship, de Beauvoir seems to be suggesting, and all these excellent characteristics disappear.

In all, none of the sexually active relationships in *The Mandarins* can in any sense be described as happy or fulfilled, and the costs to all parties, in terms of emotional turmoil, empty days, sleepless nights, and enervating misery are considerable. It is true that Anne and Lewis Brogan have their moments of romance and intense sexual satisfaction, but all the time a question hangs over their affair of how their relationship is going to develop. Lewis is perhaps understandably moody at the thought that his love for Anne can only be temporary while Anne is appalled by the prospect of years of emotional and sexual sterility with Robert, and yet is unable to relinquish her loyalties and commitments to him, Paris, and the professional life which she has established there. The best that she can offer Lewis is a permanent, yet part-time arrangement. She would return to Paris and Robert for most of the year, while continuing to spend holidays and other free time with Lewis. The idea does not appeal to Lewis, and the affair ends. The end of the affair is also very nearly the end of Anne, since she is overwhelmed by grief and contemplates suicide. But finally she achieves a kind of *modus vivendi*, she makes a conscious decision to relinquish what she decides were the false dreams and hopes which her love was based upon; in particular the illusion that love can ever provide lasting happiness:

> 'Dead is the child who believed in paradise, dead the girl who thought immortal the books, the ideas, and the man she loved, dead the young woman who walked overwhelmed through a world promised to happiness, dead the woman in love who would wake up laughing in Lewis's arms.'

(TM, 760)

The best thing to do with dreams, Anne concludes, is to bury them. The infinite promises which the world seems to offer are all illusory, particularly if they happen to be dreams of transcendence, of discovering another individual with whom one becomes one united human being. Indeed, the greater the hope of this transcendence, the more, the novel suggests, it is doomed to failure.

Yet if the final chapters of *The Mandarins* are bleak, what is offered to Anne is at least her interest in her work and the happy memories of the life which she and Robert have shared, and which they still have. Something, therefore, is still left to her, and she knows nothing except love and consideration from the men with whom she is involved. Robert and Lewis are both, in their different ways, deeply fond of her, and concerned for her welfare. Whatever the difficulties of heterosexuality, compassion, concern, and mutual companionship still exist as possibilities between men and women. But in her final novel and short stories, de Beauvoir abandons the fictional portrayal of any such possibilities, and portrays instead heterosexual relationships that are based on mutual exploitation and manipulation. Furthermore, in the three short stories that make up the collection *The Woman Destroyed*, the theme of women destroyed by love for men (the Elizabeth and Paula theme of the earlier novels) is brought to its fullest and most vivid representation in the short story 'La Femme rompue'.

Although in these final works there is a major shift towards pessimism and negative expectations about heterosexuality there is a further and equally significant development in that the milieu which de Beauvoir writes about is no longer that of the liberal, intellectual world. Instead, she places the characters in managerial or technocratic jobs, gives them quite different preoccupations from her earlier characters, and divorces them completely from the values of the previous novels. Thus in *Les Belles Images* the heroine is a woman called Laurence, who works in advertising. Her husband Jean-Charles is an architect, and quite unlike any of the previous men in de Beauvoir's fiction in that he has no ideas other than a determined commitment to industrial capitalism, which has provided him with a comfortable and secure life. He is predominantly interested in making money, acquiring the material possessions appropriate to a well-paid fashionable male, and making sure that his family life conforms to the stereotypical picture of conventional society. He does not demand from Laurence that she shares any ideal with him: what he wants is an attractive wife who does not damage his car too often.

The title of the novel is, like that of all de Beauvoir's novels, most apt. The characters are devoted to images of themselves, their motivation derives from maintaining those socially constructed fictions about how people 'like them' should behave, act, and even appear in certain circumstances. Thus Laurence arranges her pose of appropriate wifely gratitude when Jean-Charles has given her an expensive present:

> 'She bowed her head a little so that he could fasten the necklace again: a perfect picture of the couple who still adore one another after ten years of marriage. He was buying conjugal peace, the delights of the home, understanding, love; and pride in himself. She gazed at herself in the mirror. "Darling you were right to insist: I'm wild with happiness".'

(BI, 118)

Others, as much as Laurence, are conscious of the correct demeanour to adopt in particular situations and moods: one puts on the role of concerned wife, adoring mistress, anxious mother, and so on, as is demanded. All such behaviour is light years away from that of the tortured lovers of *She Came to Stay* or the deeply committed political activists of *The Mandarins*. Liberal humanism has disappeared under a barrage of affluence and consumerism, and has been replaced by what has been described as 'the consciousness of the Club Mediterranée', or thought which is attractive, not too demanding, and just different enough to be titillating (Goldmann 1970).

The attack on the consumer society and on the repressive tolerance of advanced industrial capitalism in *Les Belles Images* is, for some critics, not quite sharp enough. Whether or not they are right, the novel is convincing as a portrait of an affluent, decadent, and essentially valueless society – a society which is not necessarily immoral in any conventional sense (indeed most of the characters would be horrified by any truly unorthodox behaviour) but is quite ruthlessly without values if a concern for public, general issues is regarded as a funda-mental and essential ingredient of morality. Nobody in *Les Belles Images*, with the exception of Laurence (whom her husband regards as slightly sentimental in her views), ever has any twinges of interest or conscience in matters which do not affect their own interests. But when their own interests are attacked, they can fight with quite ferocious determination, as is illustrated by the case of Laurence's mother, Dominique. For some years, Dominique has been living with the rich and powerful Gilbert. Suddenly, Gilbert decides to abandon Dominique for a much younger woman, and in a mood of vindictive anger and spite Dominique writes to the woman, giving full details of Gilbert's past, and attempting, as far as she is able, to cast an extremely long shadow over what is left of his future. Dominique is, of course, one in the long line of de Beauvoir's heroines who become unbalanced, violent, or at least temporarily insane when abandoned by their male lover, but Dominique's reaction is both more furious (and in a way more spiteful, since it is directed against a third party) and more superficial, since she eventually recovers her composure and without any apparent sense of emotional loss continues with her life.

Emotional life for the characters in *Les Belles Images* is, as the case of Dominique demonstrates, both intense and yet largely fleeting: there is a great deal of desire, both innate and also constructed, for close personal relationships ('a woman without a man is a half-failure', says Dominique at one point) and yet many of the relationships that result from these needs are largely about the acquisition of the state of being involved with another person. A man or a woman thus becomes valued at least in part because it is socially appropriate to be married, or have a lover, or simply have 'a relationship'. Any individual characteristics that the person might have, or the shared values and views that a couple might possess, are largely subservient to the possession of a sexual partner. Inevitably, since a market-place in sexual relationships operates (and has operated for some time, and is not an invention of monopoly capitalism), it is important that the man or woman is attractive, and has the right sort of job for a particular social milieu; but more fundamental questions, the kind of questions asked in *The Mandarins* or *She Came to Stay* about moral choices or an individual's capacity for good or evil, are no longer asked.

The bleakness of personal relationships in advanced industrial capitalism has been a subject that has preoccupied many writers besides de Beauvoir.[1] The loss of the sense of individual commitment to others, the contradictory demands within the family of the man, the woman and the children, and the increasing penetration of all areas of social and personal life by economic and material values have all contributed to a situation in which individual, long-term relationships seem increasingly redundant. Given that many of the social constraints (other than material ones) on remarriage and divorce have disappeared or lessened, it is now perfectly possible for individuals to exchange one partner for another, to say of a human being, as one might of an object, that she or he is 'past its best' or can no longer satisfy a certain set of desires. But as de Beauvoir rightly perceives, this situation is not the equal preserve of the sexes: she had always identified the problem of women abandoned by men; now, in *Les Belles Images* and more significantly in *The Woman Destroyed*, she identifies the culture in which people become objects, but the objects least able to manipulate their fate are women. The consumer society is, therefore, a general background, but its effects are far from equally distributed between the sexes.

In *The Woman Destroyed*, and especially in the short story which bears the same name, de Beauvoir continues her theme of the woman who has given all for a man, and is deserted by him. Monique, the heroine of *The Woman Destroyed*, is now in her forties, and is told by her husband, Maurice, that he is having an affair with another woman. At first, Monique decides to tolerate the relationship, remain the understanding and loving wife, and hope that Maurice will come back to her. As the story continues, it becomes increasingly obvious that Maurice is going to do no such thing: his lover, Noëllie, satisfies all his current desires for a chic, cosmopolitan woman of the world, just as Monique once wholly satisfied his need for a loving and supporting wife who was prepared to provide the emotional stability and reassurance wanted by a man in the early stages of a demanding professional career.

Maurice does not emerge from *The Woman Destroyed* as a sympathetic or likeable character; on the contrary he is, like Jean-Charles in *Les Belles Images*, obsessed by professional success and the establishment and gratification of his own self-image. But de Beauvoir's argument is not that all men are necessarily corrupt, or bad, or the enemy of women, although they can certainly act like that. Her point remains that although women are often the victims of male behaviour, they themselves construct the conditions of their own victimization. Monique, just as much as Paula in *The Mandarins*, deludes herself into supposing that she can live simply through the love of a man, and that in sacrificing her time, her energy, and even on occasion her own values, she has a right to expect total commitment in return. So de Beauvoir is not suggesting an analysis in which men are wrong, and women are right, but a much more complicated pattern in which men and women construct their own mutual self-destruction. Women therefore abandon all for the man they love, men accept this abandonment and self-abasement, since a particular culture accepts that that is a fitting pattern for male/female relations. The price for both sexes is, however, high. Women are never able to develop any capacity for independent or autonomous thought or action, since everything must be done with reference to the beloved. Men are trapped by guilt and social pressures into maintaining relationships that are no longer in any way rewarding.

Many contemporary feminists might argue that the situation of male independence and female dependence is one in which men are always the privileged sex, and women always the losers. De Beauvoir does not attempt to maintain this absolute dichotomy, however, and she suggests in all her novels that both sexes suffer from the excessive commitments demanded of women in love. Her existentialist values do not in fact disappear, and she maintains throughout her work a belief in individual freedom and an individual capacity for the choice of freedom. But what does change during her career as a writer, between *She Came to Stay* and *The Woman Destroyed*, is her presentation of the extent to which men and women, and particularly women, can choose their fate. Between the active, morally assertive Françoise of *She Came to Stay* and the passive suffering of Monique of *The Woman Destroyed* there is a vast distance in the range of human action; perhaps there is also a major difference in de Beauvoir's view of the relative freedoms of men and women.

Again, it is important to emphasize that de Beauvoir is not saying what some radical feminists might say – that men are free, and women unfree. In all her novels she shows that men and women are both constrained by social pressures. If Maurice in *The Woman Destroyed* is free in the formal sense of being able to leave his wife to live with a mistress, he is far from genuinely free in that he has to maintain all the appropriate poses of the professional man, the lover to his mistress, and the man with a 'great love' for another woman to the world at large. With his mistress, as de Beauvoir suggests, he is even less free than with his wife, since he has to be able to match all her expectations of professional distinction, sexual competence, and social sophistication. Compared to the agonies of heartache endured by Monique at her husband's departure this price might not seem particularly high to some readers, but de Beauvoir is showing us that there are costs, albeit different ones, for both sexes in sexual relations as they are now constituted.

Yet as we have seen, a shift has occurred, between *She Came to Stay* and *The Woman Destroyed*, in social values about human relationships, and it is possible that the loss of liberal, humanist values in the world after the Second World War has intensified patriarchy. In many ways, of course, evidence would suggest an increasing emancipation of women – better contraception, more widely available abortion, increased access to education and paid work, all these changes could be construed as improvements in the lot of women. But at the same time as these changes have taken place (and their impact has been far from universal or complete even in north-west Europe) other changes in the social construction of sexuality have arguably brought about a deterioration in the status and situation of women, in that the demands on them have increased. De Beauvoir suggests in *The Woman Destroyed* and *Les Belles Images* that the old image of the 'home-making' woman no longer accords with the myths and fantasies of a technocratic society. It is now demanded that women should be – to produce an exaggerated stereotype – brilliant brain surgeons, superb cooks, wonderful wives and mothers, and active socialites. Sexually attractive (and constantly available), intellectually able, and socially popular, the woman of the dream world of technocratic patriarchy inevitably fails to exist, except in the smallest number of cases. But like all myths, the potency of this dream lies not in its fulfilment, but in the measure it represents for reality. Thus the woman who fails to meet all, or some, of the expected attributes of the super-woman is seen as a failure, and a failure in a society which values success very highly. As Monique in *The Woman Destroyed* quite rightly perceives, the attraction of Noëllie is not her intrinsic moral qualities, but the way in which she meets Maurice's fantasies of the bright, active, professionally successful woman. That Noëllie is bright and active about issues that are not of any intrinsic value in a general political or social sense is of no concern to Maurice; what he admires is the reassurance of success and socially recognized competence. As Monique realizes, the activities to which she has devoted herself, the care of their children and the establishment and running of a home, are now dismissed as unimportant and time wasting. The care of children and housework have no material value, and are thus easily dismissed by a society in which all social relations and all work are increasingly assessed in terms of the market-place. Just as it was once a matter of status for a man to have a wife whom he could support economically, so it now becomes a matter of equal importance for a man to have a wife who 'achieves' and can demonstrate skills that have a market value. This change is, however, complex as far as its repercussions for women are concerned: on the one hand it encourages them to seek economic independence from their husbands or male others, while on the other it adds to the res-ponsibilities (including child care and the maintenance of the household) which women are deemed to bear.

De Beauvoir would no doubt see that within this change there exists the possibility for the emancipation of women from an exclusive identification with the household. Nevertheless she also acknowledges that entry into paid labour does not, in itself, guarantee any great extension in women's freedom. The question then remains of what else has to change before women can leave that state of emotional dependence on men that was so widely condemned in *The Second Sex* and illustrated in the fiction. One answer that might be introduced – that women should abandon sexual relationships with men and choose either chastity or what contemporary feminism describes as 'political lesbianism' – is categorically rejected by de Beauvoir, who writes:

> 'All feminists agree that love and sexuality must be redefined. But some of them deny that men have any part to play in a woman's life, particularly in her sexual life, whereas others wish to keep a place for them in their lives and in their beds. I side with them. I utterly revolt at the idea of shutting women up in a feminine ghetto.'

(ASD, 493)

So heterosexuality is to continue, even if 'love and sexuality' must be redefined.

In de Beauvoir's fiction we do not find, and can hardly expect to find, a programme for this redefinition of heterosexuality. Suggestions about alterations in male/female relationships are given, albeit briefly, in the conclusion to *The Second Sex*, but these remain essentially superficial and are largely related to changes in ideology. The material world, as much in *The Second Sex* as in the fiction, is largely a background (albeit sometimes an inconvenient one) against which individuals attempt to work out their metaphysical differences. So most of the campaigns of contemporary feminism for equal participation in work and child care by men and women, for equal pay for the sexes, and for the ending of discriminatory legislation against women find little place in de Beauvoir's work. That is not to say that she would condemn any of the changes – on the contrary, she has consistently advocated the majority of them – but that she undervalues the part that these issues play in the determination of a woman's (or a man's) life. But most striking of all is the absence in de Beauvoir's fiction of any discussion of women as mothers or men as fathers. It is true that Anne in *The Mandarins* has a daughter, and Monique in *The Woman Destroyed* has two daughters, but these relationships between fictional mothers and daughters is, at best, distant. What is missing from the account of male/female relations, and the lives of both sexes, is a portrayal of the desire to bear children, and the costs and rewards of being a parent. None of the men in the novels has anything to do with children; Robert and Perron in *The Mandarins* have fleeting encounters with their offspring, but family life in any significant sense is not part of their experience.

Such a portrayal of men's relationships with their children can hardly be described as entirely unrealistic. Numerous feminists have pointed out that many men have little to do with their children and that the burden of child care falls almost exclusively on women. So what is interesting about de Beauvoir's account of maternity and paternity is that it is markedly matter of fact: children are sometimes simply in existence but apparently constitute little of emotional significance. Monique is attached to her children, yet they offer little compensation for the loss of Maurice; Anne is often irritated and appalled by Nadine's behaviour but generally adopts towards her an attitude of complete objectivity. The central female characters of the novels never express their attitudes towards their own mothers: strong, assertive, and (in the case of Françoise and Anne) independent women arrive in the world and in the novels with little or no explanation of why they should have those characteristics and why they are so markedly different from the miserably dependent Monique or Paula. Why, we might ask, do the daughters of Monique turn out to be so different – the one traditional and the other aggressively independent and assertive? Equally, there is little explanation for the constant, often spiteful, delinquency of Nadine. Certainly, a previous lover had been killed during the war, but this scarcely explains the petty vindictiveness of her behaviour towards other women – particularly Paula and Anne.

But this feature of *The Mandarins*, that is the behaviour of Nadine towards Anne and Paula, illustrates particularly clearly an important and striking feature of de Beauvoir's fiction: that women do not, on the whole, behave particularly well towards each other. When a man is involved with two women, or a woman is involved in competition for a particular man, women act markedly badly. Quite how badly varies from murdering the other woman in *She Came to Stay*, to coquetry and competitive sexuality in the case of Nadine in *The Mandarins* or Noëllie in *The Woman Destroyed*. This feature of de Beauvoir's fiction departs from a general feature of much fiction written by women, in which women, and especially sisters, are bound together by ties of loyalty and concern. For example, Austen and Eliot do not always show women who are well disposed towards each other (competition for men reaches heights of intensity and moral compromise in Austen's *Mansfield Park* and *Sense and Sensibility*) but they do show women who are capable of genuine and even, on occasions, unselfish concern for other women. It is interesting that de Beauvoir quotes a male author – Tolstoy – to illustrate a point about women's lack of common identity, and uses, from the fiction of women authors, only examples which suggest female independence (Maggie Tulliver of *The Mill on the Floss* or Jo of *Little Women*) or female enslavement (the women portrayed by Colette). There is no mention of the altruism of Dorothea in *Middlemarch*, with her real generosity of spirit towards the clinging and vapid Rosamond, or the quiet moral strength of Anne in *Persuasion*, who is capable of acknowledging the freedom of the man whom she still loves to choose another woman. These women do not act as 'the other' but very much as individuals who have confronted and accepted the possibilities of women's capacity for moral choice and action. Even if they are constrained within circumstances that none of de Beauvoir's heroines knows, they nevertheless show an alternative to the assumptions that de Beauvoir has made about women, in that they do not blindly follow accepted standards and conventions, and are, most importantly, prepared to make the kind of moral decision that promises neither security nor comfort nor male approbation.

To read literature as de Beauvoir does in *The Second Sex* is largely to ignore the assertiveness of which women have been shown to be capable. This does not answer the question of whether or not literature is in any sense a mirror of reality, but it does suggest that there exists an alternative perception to the dominant ideology of male power and female powerlessness. Increasingly, women's 'resistance' has been discovered by historians and literary critics, and this recent discovery of the female past has alerted many people against assuming that what is taken as the 'great' literary tradition or the conventional version of history is necessarily a comprehensive or even accurate view.[2] In the case of de Beauvoir's novels we have to ask, therefore, if they do not reflect, in a fictional form, some of the generalizations about male power and female powerlessness that are outlined in *The Second Sex*. Given that this is the theme that informs de Beauvoir's novels, we must ask next how adequate de Beauvoir's novels are in their portrayal of individual personal relationships between the sexes. In terms of what could be described as 'feminist realism' and its judgements about literature, de Beauvoir's fiction would be hightly rated, since she shows in fictional terms precisely those aspects of female emotional dependence on men which feminists have for so long attacked. Equally, de Beauvoir portrays the different standards of sexual morality that exist for men and women, and provides more than one instance of men's lack of interest in certain fundamental aspects of women's existence. For example, the unfaithful Maurice in *The Woman Destroyed* takes no interest, or part in, the home which he has been so content to enjoy.

But while de Beauvoir's fiction passes this test of portraying what is assumed to be a reality of male power and female subservience, it is also necessary to ask if she adequately portrays some of the complexities of motivation and compromise which are a feature of many people's lives. Literature would be very dull if it were about the humdrum daily life which never involved choice or change, but de Beauvoir does suggest a world in which emotional life is always active and always a matter of idealized choice. Wives and husbands do not stay together because of material necessity, let alone for 'the sake of the children', and all the characters act with a complete lack of interest in the material circumstances of their individual choices. Money, as almost all the great European novelists have appreciated, is an important, if not a determining, feature of human existence, and few characters of this tradition are shown without some reference to the means by which they acquire their livelihood and maintain themselves. Further, as was so well portrayed by Eliot, Austen, the Brontës, Flaubert, and Mann, money made the person: men and women were not born with grace, or ease, or perfect composure, these attributes were provided by a culture which was in its turn created by wealth. Emma Bovary was not attracted to the facile Roland for any reason other than those aspects of his person which had, in a very real sense, been bought. Whatever the virtues of the homely Charles Bovary, they counted for nothing in his wife's eyes against his rough manners and untutored behaviour. Emma, like many other heroines, could find what she thought was 'love' and 'beauty' in the sight of expensive clothes and the acquisitions of wealth.

This aspect of women's behaviour, their interest in what men can provide for them in material terms and what men themselves appear as in terms of the material world, is a feature of male/female relations that is largely absent from de Beauvoir's world. Only in *The Woman Destroyed*, in the portrayal of Maurice and Noëllie, do we find it suggested that human beings do not make abstract, individualized judgements about each other, but that social values and aspirations are an extremely important part of sexual relations. In the other novels, judgements about others, the affection of one for another, are about the characteristics of the individual and those characteristics alone. The problem, of course, is that no individual exists in such a highly individualized sense, and it is not, therefore, either cynical or materially over-deterministic to point out that what individuals can love or value in each other has often little to do with the other person but a great deal to do with the projection of individual needs or aspirations on to another. The way in which women would project on to men their own needs, and the possibilities for the realization of what they wished to become, was expressed very clearly by a number of nineteenth-century female novelists. George Eliot in particular brilliantly portrayed the way in which women would locate in men what they themselves wanted. Seldom in fiction has the bending of one will to another been more accurately portrayed than in the depiction in *Middlemarch* of the courtship betwen Lydgate and Rosamond Vincy. Lydgate has no wish to marry Rosamond, Rosamond has absolutely no interest in Lydgate's ideas or aspirations. And yet:

> 'she looked at Lydgate and the tears fell over her cheeks. There
> could have been no more complete answer than that silence, and
> Lydgate, forgetting everything else, completely mastered by the
> onrush of tenderness and the feeling that this sweet young
> creature depended on him for her joy, actually put his arms
> around her, folding her gently and protectingly; he was used to
> being gentle with the weak and the suffering.'[3]

From that moment on, Lydgate is the hopeless captive of Rosamond's
whims. He can no more refuse to concede her wishes than he can fly,
and although he may occasionally vent his dissatisfactions in ill
humour he cannot in any substantial sense act as a free man.

Yet many feminists would point out, here, that a measure of
Rosamond's lack of freedom, and dependence on men, is that she has to
make men do what she wants for her, since she is incapable of achieving
her own aims through her own efforts. Petit-bourgeois women in
nineteenth-century Europe could not establish a household or a secure
place in society without a husband – men had a social as well as an
economic function as far as women were concerned. That they have not
lost this function is an endless complaint of contemporary feminism. A
woman without a man may be like a fish without a bicycle in terms of
political slogans, but in terms of social reality a woman without a
husband is generally poor, and her children are certainly regarded as
illegitimate. Attachment to men, and confirmation by men, is therefore
as much now as in the nineteenth century a feature of women's
existence. Given that this is the case and was the case when de Beauvoir
wrote her fiction, what remains interesting about her novels is the way
in which she constructs the attraction that men have for women.
Material provision is not given prominence, neither is sexuality. She
shows in *She Came to Stay*, *The Blood of Others*, and *The Mandarins* how
men and women might be bound together by rational and political ties,
but still the issue remains of what the sexes want from each other that
they cannot gain from members of their own sex. In the relationships
that seem to be offered as the most developed and fulfilled (Françoise
and Pierre of *She Came to Stay*, and Anne and Robert Dubreuilh of *The
Mandarins*) sexuality is absent, and what exists between the two parties
is a long-standing friendship that might equally well exist between two
men or two women, and might be less likely to entail the kind of
jealousies, drama, and high passions that beset these two couples. It is,
perhaps, a reflection on the undeveloped state of the intellectual and
political lives of most women that exceptional women (the Françoise or

Anne of intellectual/Bohemian life) can only gain from men the kind of companionship that they seek? But if this is the case, we must also ask if the power that men have over women in the novels of de Beauvoir is no longer a power of economic dominance or superior social standing, but the possession of intellectual and mental power. The symbolic phallic power of Robert of *The Mandarins* and Pierre of *She Came to Stay* is not, therefore, the same as it might be for women with more conventional domestic and reproductive ambitions, but it is nevertheless power – an ability to offer the kind of coherent understanding of the world which women themselves are never portrayed as capable of. That is not to say that they are not competent, hard working, talented, and capable – in the cases of Hélène of *The Blood of Others* or Françoise of *She Came to Stay* – of brave and determined action, but that they do not possess the same capacities for coherence and the systematization of the social world as the men with whom they are associated.

The temptation, at this point, to shift from a discussion of de Beauvoir's fiction to a discussion of de Beauvoir's relationship with Sartre is very strong. So much of de Beauvoir's fiction is autobiographical that it is difficult not to see the positive relationships between men and women in her fiction as fictional portrayals of her own life with Sartre. *She Came to Stay* is openly admitted as autobiographical. *The Mandarins* contains endless examples of people and places whom de Beauvoir has described in either *The Prime of Life* or *Force of Circumstance*. It is impossible not to read de Beauvoir for Anne in *The Mandarins*, or Sartre for Robert in the novel. Nevertheless, the temptation to list the similarities between fact and fiction will be resisted, not the least because it is a commonplace of fiction that novelists tend to write about the people and the circumstances that they know best (and generally write badly when they try and write about cultures that are foreign to them – as in the case of de Beauvoir in her *All Men Are Mortal*). What is interesting about the relations between men and women in de Beauvoir's fiction is not, therefore, how far it follows the details of her own experience but how the organization, and fictional portrayal, of reality in her novels can be said to be patriarchal or feminist. The issue, then, is whether she shows male/female relations in ways that are genuinely illuminating and progressive, or merely suggestive of ways in which women might be more like men, and measure more nearly that independent woman who dominates the conclusion of *The Second Sex*.

The case for the patriarchal nature of de Beauvoir's novels is that they show women as more fulfilled, and only able to be free in any significant sense, when they follow closely male patterns of professional commitment. Further it has to be said that although de Beauvoir is very accurate in her portrayal of female weaknesses – their dependence and deviousness in particular – she is less than equally critical in her portrayal of men. She does not condemn Pierre for his infatuation with Xavière in *She Came to Stay*, nor is it suggested that this man who was held up as a model of moral strength and integrity must have been less than perfectly perceived and understood if he is now capable of a consuming passion for someone as transparently anxious to test her powers of sexual attraction as Xavière. Nor is Robert condemned for the emotional distance and detachment that almost drive Anne into Lewis's arms: if she perceives her life as emotionally sterile and less than happy, it does not seem implausible that she might question Robert's relationship to her rather than seeking another man, and eventually causing both him and herself a good deal of pain. But Robert's preoccupation is never questioned, and here is to be found an instance of an unthinking acceptance of patriarchal ideology: that it is perfectly legitimate, even admirable, for men to be so much concerned with their careers, or political ambitions, or whatever else, that they have no time for emotional life. Indeed, part of Anne's admiration for Robert is that he is committed and preoccupied – yet she does not connect this preoccupation with the lack of satisfaction of her own needs or her joy in meeting Lewis. Nor is any connection ever made in the novel between Nadine's delinquency and her petty and selfish seeking for attention, and the professional commitments of her parents. It is a commonplace of anti-feminism that women are always blamed for the failures and failings of their children, but at no point does de Beauvoir ever examine this or suggest that Nadine's desire for male attention and confirmation might have some roots both in the distance between her and her father, and in the model offered to her by her mother of the 'successful' woman, a person indistinguishable, in certain crucial respects, from the successful professional male. Neither parent in the Dubreuilh household can have offered a great deal in terms of emotional engagement, identification, or warmth.

So apparently 'good' men in de Beauvoir's fiction are men who are emotionally distant from their children, or capable of infatuation that harms others, or too self-absorbed to question the commitment of others to them – as is the case of Henri in *The Mandarins*. What this illustrates is the long-standing dichotomy which the west has made between public men and private women – if men are to be assessed as 'good' then this is done largely in terms of their public lives. There has always been an excellent case for keeping the long arm of the state and public morality away from the private lives of citizens, yet feminism has raised, as much now as in its earlier days, the question of how morality, or moral standing, is to be assessed. Clearly, de Beauvoir might well regard Robert as a 'good' man, yet a contemporary feminist might say that no man, whatever his political and public virtues, could be regarded as 'good' while he was so neglectful of the emotional needs of his wife and daughter. Thus again we find that de Beauvoir reflects male standards and assumptions in her assessment of what constitutes virtue. Pierre and Robert emerge as morally acceptable even if the former has, through his infidelity, caused immense suffering, and the latter has been guilty, if not of sins of commission, then at least of sins of omission. Care for others (in a more than cerebral sense) and a personal commitment not to an abstract ideal of 'freedom' but to another person, whose feelings affect one's actions, are not always features of the 'good' men of de Beauvoir's world.

That the moral worlds and moral standards of men and women are not the same has now become a common observation of contemporary feminism. The importance of a man's behaviour in his private world has become widely accepted, and although none of the men in de Beauvoir's fiction ranks as an out-and-out villain, some of them do not meet the exacting, or different, standards that feminism has now introduced into our understanding of morality. It is arguable that the stress which feminism lays on private behaviour (often summed up in the slogan 'the personal is political') sometimes entails the danger that public questions may be overlooked: a stress on individual behaviour at the cost of the consideration of the actions of the collectivity. But this is not a charge that could be levelled against de Beauvoir: whatever the shortcomings, or determinants, of her view of morality – either in the real world or as portrayed in her novels – she has often acted with courage and determination in stating her political convictions. That these convictions have often been unpopular, and made it difficult for her to live in her own country, will be discussed in the following chapter. In real life, therefore, she has been an example of the way in which women are as capable as men of moral and political conviction. That example is, perhaps, her most lasting contribution to feminism.

5
_____Politics and problems_____

De Beauvoir has claimed that commentators on her work have over-emphasized her discussions of the relationship between the sexes in such a way that other aspects of her work have been obscured.[1] In particular she has argued that what has often been overlooked is her discussion of political issues and problems. This view is interesting in that de Beauvoir fails to ask why this might have been the case, or to draw any implications from the lack of interest of critics in her political writing. There are, however, various reasons why critics have not been interested in her political writing – among them the misogyny that believes that women have nothing serious to say about politics, and equally the capacity of many critics to concentrate on what is sensational about an author's work. Thus a discussion of abortion and sexuality was sensational in France in 1949 in a way that de Beauvoir's accounts of the United States or China were not.

But there are, of course, in addition to these reasons others which are less flattering to de Beauvoir. Most particularly, it has to be asked if de Beauvoir contributed anything of interest to political discussions. Certainly, *The Second Sex* constitutes a major contribution to the discussion of the politics of sexuality and sexual difference, but the issue remains of de Beauvoir's understanding of the political world in the widest sense. In particular, what has to be questioned is de Beauvoir's understanding of the structure of social life. *The Second Sex* ends with a call to women to participate more fully in social life, but the model of the social world that this call invokes is one in which 'women' or 'the family' form distinct areas of social existence, removed from 'the state' or other institutional structures. Indeed, the model of the social world that organizes *The Second Sex* recalls the structural functionalism of Talcott Parsons; moreover, it is a model which de Beauvoir retains throughout her work. Thus in an interview in 1977 de Beauvoir spoke of the importance of women organizing for themselves, 'independent of the class struggle'. She continued in conversation with Alice Jardine:

> 'A.J.: What goal should women work for today?
> S.B.: Essentially, for the women's revolution. But if it were accomplished, it would, at the same time, shake society.'
>
> (Jardine 1979)

The problem with this – apart from the major difficulty that women, since they are social beings, can never be entirely independent of the class structure – is twofold. First, it has to be asked if all women, regardless of characteristics of class or race, share the same interests. Second, we must ask if women were to organize 'for the women's revolution' how the changes brought about would affect that entity defined by de Beauvoir as 'society'. Certainly, the specific form of the sexual division of labour would be changed, but that is quite different from supposing that capitalism, or state socialism, would be fundamentally shaken. Reorganized, altered, even improved – these are certainties, but fundamentally changed remains another question. It therefore has to be asked if de Beauvoir does not articulate the view (later expressed by feminists such as Mary Daly or Adrienne Rich) that women's politics are inevitably 'good' in the sense of being left wing, liberal, or progressive.

This issue should not obscure, or be interpreted as an attack on, the integrity, consistency, and sincerity of de Beauvoir's political views and statements: as suggested at the conclusion of the previous chapter de Beauvoir has never been a closet socialist or failed to make difficult and dangerous political gestures. On the contrary, her opposition to the politics of the French government in Algeria in the period of decolonization in the 1950s brought her and Sartre into considerable odium with their fellow citizens. Sartre's flat was bombed and de Beauvoir was threatened with similar attacks. For whatever reason – the misogynist gallantry of the French, or the greater threat posed by Sartre – it was always Sartre who was the subject of more serious attack, but de Beauvoir shared to the full the verbal and written abuse of those who were opposed to an independent Algeria. Similarly, in the 1970s de Beauvoir spoke out in favour of the legalization of abortion in France and in doing so identified herself as a woman who had had an abortion. These two instances should be sufficient to clear de Beauvoir of the charge that she has failed either to take a stand on issues of conscience or to lend her prestige and fame to causes that involve the decrease of privilege. When she, and other women, signed the *Manifeste de 343* (a manifesto signed by 343 women who had themselves had abortions), it was apparent that what was at stake was not simply the possibility of the termination of pregnancy, but the extension of that possibility to those outside the cosmopolitan and well-connected circle of women who made up the group of '343'.

So both in her political actions and in her mode of life, de Beauvoir can be seen as a perfect democrat in that she has neither claimed privilege nor worked for its continuation. Her way of life has always been unostentatious: a small flat, simple clothes, and an apparent long-standing loyalty to family and to friends of the past. Indeed, a substantial section of *All Said and Done* documents de Beauvoir's continuing association with, and interest in, the people who shared her youth and obscure early maturity. This is not a human being who has chosen the company of the famous, or sought out celebrity. Both *Force of Circumstance* and *All Said and Done*, the volumes of autobiography which cover de Beauvoir's years as an internationally known woman of letters, attest to the fact that although de Beauvoir numbered among her friends and acquaintances the rich, the famous, and the powerful, she also spent a good deal of time with what she describes as her 'family' – the long-standing friends Olga and Bost, and others who had shared the years of obscurity. *All Said and Done* contains, in addition, a long discussion of de Beauvoir's young friend Sylvie le Bon, a student whom she befriended. Inevitably, de Beauvoir's account of her life after 1945 is sprinkled with references to conversations with Picasso, Castro, Ehrenberg, Giacometti, Camus, Koestler, and other political and artistic giants of the twentieth century but at the same time her autobiography attests to an existence which remained rooted in a precisely located and domestic setting.

Nevertheless whilst de Beauvoir's account of her social life reveals both the domestic simplicity of her existence, and the friendship network of the European intelligentsia, it also demonstrates her isolation from institutional life of any kind. Perhaps for a writer this was bound to be the case, but for a writer with political convictions and, from the 1950s onwards, a writer with an increasingly political message, it is a marked omission. Thus we find in de Beauvoir few accounts of meetings, of committees, of organization, or of any of the other humdrum associations of political life. De Beauvoir's politics were essentially those of intellectual intervention – the statement, the manifesto – rather than engagement with other individuals in organizations and institutions. Hence what emerges from de Beauvoir's pen is unmediated by practical political life: her politics are fierce and brave and faultlessly progressive but they do not emerge out of a life lived in institutional politics.

Concomitant with this feature of de Beauvoir's life and work, two points must be made. First, it must be reiterated that no criticism is intended of the nature of de Beauvoir's life: she chose to be a writer, an intellectual, rather than a politician. So the point of a consideration of her way of life is not to criticize, but to illuminate the nature of her politics and her attitude to social intervention and the possibility of social change. The second point is that de Beauvoir epitomizes what is sometimes construed as the dilemma of the relationship of the intellectual to politics. Thus critics (of both the left and the right) condemn writers and intellectuals as divorced from social reality or separated from the 'real' concerns of the 'ordinary' world. Such critics, as well as invoking a model of the world which rigidly separates thought from action, tend to overlook the importance that the state attaches to the opinions of writers and intellectuals. The works of Thomas Mann and Solzhenitsyn were burned or banned precisely because the printed word does matter and is construed as important. But the view that intellectuals are remote from 'real life' has been stated most fully in the case of de Beauvoir by Anne Whitmarsh, who writes that:

> 'support for the Left, vigilance and criticism of the system are
> really not enough to overthrow society. . . . in fact if everyone
> acted like Simone de Beauvoir very few changes would ever take
> place in society. She wishes society to alter radically and sees that
> action must be taken to bring this about, but she has been happy
> for most of her life to leave this to other people.'
>
> (Whitmarsh 1981)

So the charge here is that de Beauvoir, whatever her expressed opinions in print, has played an insufficient part in *realpolitik*: she has not chosen the politics of the platform, the committee meeting, or the organized party.

On the other hand, what de Beauvoir has done is to act consistently as a political writer, in that from her earliest existential novels her writing has been motivated by political convictions and values. So although Whitmarsh is perfectly correct in pointing out de Beauvoir's distance from organized, practical politics, the theme of this chapter is not structured by a belief in the apolitical, or the inadequately political, nature of de Beauvoir's work. It is not that her politics are inadequate, rather that they are in some crucial respects limited and essentially conservative. But another value must also be asserted here: the value of the written word. In criticizing de Beauvoir for her limited engagement with practical politics Whitmarsh takes what I would argue is a misguided view of politics: that politics are only about organized political action and not about the written word, the critique of existing society, or the intellectual intervention and/or dispute. Many political movements, many changes in the lives of numerous citizens have taken place because of activity in the apparently remote and isolated academic's study. So what is at stake here is the question of the validity of what de Beauvoir wrote; the issue is that of whether or not her analysis, both of relations between the sexes and of western social life in general, is adequate as a focus for debate about the change of those relations and that social system. It must also be said, as a matter of empirical fact, that de Beauvoir did devote some time and energy to politics – writing a study of torture in Algeria (*Djamila Boupacha*) and taking part, with Sartre, in the Russell War Crimes Tribunal during the years of United States military intervention in South-East Asia.

De Beauvoir's early training and early commitment, as already discussed in Chapter 2, were in, and to, philosophy and the discussion through fiction of the moral dilemmas of individuals. The inadequacies of existentialism as a system of morality were rapidly realized by de Beauvoir, and after the Second World War she adopted a far more explicitly political stance. This is not to say that her existentialist novels or her philosophical essays were strictly speaking apolitical, but politics in this period were conceived of essentially in terms of personal choice. What de Beauvoir's work from this period demonstrates is an understanding of personal choice as a matter of politics: de Beauvoir argues for choice that is motivated by a particular view of freedom, namely that freedom and the responsibility to choose are almost synonymous. The unfree, the amoral person is, to de Beauvoir at this point, the person who fails to acknowledge that an essential part of their humanity is their ability to choose, and to allow others to do the same. Some of the absurdities of this position – in particular its total irrelevance in situations in which coercion and large-scale social and political power were brought into play – were admitted by Sartre and de Beauvoir from the beginning of the Second World War. But what never seemed to vanish from de Beauvoir's work was a belief in the power of the individual to choose, and by implication the absolute autonomy of the individual both from society in the general sense and from social life in the more personal sense of a biography and a personal history.

This issue in de Beauvoir's work raises an interesting and important question for both socialists and feminists. De Beauvoir belongs to a tradition in which individual choice is allowed prime place: educate or inform individuals 'properly' (in de Beauvoir's view this would mean educating them on the need for feminism or socialism) and they will then embrace that cause. So what has to be done is a task, albeit massive, of enlightenment and education. Tell the world about socialism and feminism, and both will result, since people will be in a position to 'choose' the correct analysis. The difficulty with this position is that it overlooks the not inconsiderable problem of the complexities of human interests and associations. To take a concrete example: *The Second Sex* invites women to reject passivity and to assert their independence and autonomy. The advice is excellent if it can be taken for granted that the assertion of independence by one individual is not the loss of independence for another. Moreover, it may well be the case that independence is only of value in a society and in a culture which enforces ties of dependence and control. In the bourgeois society which de Beauvoir attacks in *The Second Sex* independence for women makes perfect sense, since it liberates them from the claims of social convention and patriarchal social control. But in other societies, or in other cultures within bourgeois society, independence makes no sense, and has no value, since the strength of individuals lies not in their individual achievements (or their inherent capacity for them) but in their ties with others and in networks of mutual support and sympathy. Equally, when de Beauvoir calls for greater female independence what she is also calling for is an independence that permits greater communication with the (male) other. Arguing that emotional and sexual relationships between men and women have been distorted by a dialectic of female passivity and male aggression and assertiveness, de Beauvoir argues for an alternative model of heterosexual intimacy, but one still based on the affirmation of individual identity through another individual. And this affirmation is best, indeed only, achieved through relationships between people of opposite sex.

De Beauvoir's attitude to eroticism and sexuality is such that she can only fully endorse heterosexuality. The passages in *The Second Sex* which deal with lesbianism suggest a somewhat stereotypical view of lesbian relationships – 'many athletic women are homosexual' writes de

Beauvoir (SS, 385). Moreover, she takes what would now be regarded as a heterosexist attitude to homosexual relationships, assuming that they must conform to the pattern of an active (male) partner and a passive (female) partner. She writes that the active lesbian partner will:

> 'adopt a masculine attitude in part to repudiate any appearance of complicity with (submissive) women; she forms with a feminine woman companion a couple in which she represents the male person: play-acting that is, indeed, a "masculine protest".'
>
> (SS, 385)

But even if the relationship forms a conventional pattern it is unlikely to be successful. Nothing, de Beauvoir argues, can overcome the essential hostility that women feel towards each other:

> 'A man and a woman are intimidated by the fact that they are different: he feels pity and concern for her . . . she respects him and fears him somewhat. . . . But women are pitiless toward each other; they thwart, provoke, pursue, fall upon one another tooth and nail, and drag each other down into bottomless abjection . . . between two women tears and frenzies rise in alternate crescendo; their appetite for outdoing each other in reproaches and for endlessly "having it out" is insatiable. Demands, recriminations, jealousy, tyrannizing – all these plagues of married life are here let loose with redoubled intensity.'

Since lesbian relationships are, for de Beauvoir, such an unsatis-factory alternative to heterosexuality, what she wishes to put in the place of conventional (active/passive) heterosexuality is the freely chosen eroticism endorsed in *The Second Sex*. It is a view which de Beauvoir was later to elaborate in an essay on Brigitte Bardot. Writing of Bardot's sexuality, de Beauvoir praised her for what she regarded as her fearless statement of female sexual desire: 'The male is an object to her, just as she is to him. . . . To spurn jewels and cosmetics and high heels and girdles is to refuse to transform oneself into a remote idol' (BB, 20–1).

So what emerges from de Beauvoir's arguments on independence and independent sexuality for women is a blueprint for sexual relations that it is now difficult not to see as an argument premised on the belief of the transforming and transcending power of the heterosexual orgasm. As Jeffrey Weeks – and others – have pointed out such arguments are typical of the tradition of sexual libertarianism, a tradition which accepts without question the central importance of

heterosexual intercourse (Weeks 1981: Chapter 13). And it is interesting that despite her rejection of Engels, de Beauvoir's hopes for the
new, independent female sexuality that will be released by women's
economic and emotional emancipation are very similar to his: he wrote
in 1884 of his hopes for a 'gradual rise of more unrestrained sexual
intercourse' that would follow from women's entry into social production (Engels 1967).

It is by now apparent that women's entry into paid work does not *per
se* constitute a condition for their emancipation. So it remains the case
that de Beauvoir's call for the economic independence and autonomy
of women is only relevant, as a condition of female emancipation, to
those women in a position which allows them to benefit from the
possibilities of paid work. For women for whom the context and
conditions of social production ensure that paid work is far from
emancipation in the sense understood by de Beauvoir, or for women
whose understanding of sexuality is less specifically and solely
heterosexual, there is less offered by de Beauvoir's analysis.
Nevertheless, since de Beauvoir is also offering a morality about
sexuality, it is important to ask if her discussion of a possible alternative
morality of sexuality is of use.

De Beauvoir, as suggested in earlier chapters, rejects conventional sexual morality. She does not endorse marriage, or formal,
institutionalized relationships between individuals. Nor does she, like
later feminists, suggest that conventional morality is to be damned
because it is sex specific. Her objections to conventional morality are
that it limits genuine choice, and is liable to imprison the individual in a
web of lies and evasions. As we have seen, to de Beauvoir morality is
valueless when it is guided by the passive acceptance of conventional
expectations and assumptions. So the individual is placed at the centre
of de Beauvoir's moral universe: she or he must choose, or sacrifice
their claim to true and valid humanity. But, and here arises the
problem for socialists and feminists alike, the placing of the individual
at the centre of the moral universe allows very little room for a discussion of the social implications of individual decisions. Nor does
it allow that in accepting the moral imperative of choosing choice, some
individuals are much better placed than others to choose certain
options. There is, for example, very little sense in which an unmarried,
poor, 16-year-old girl 'chooses' an abortion: she has few other viable
options. Equally, if that same 16-year-old girl chose not to terminate
her pregnancy, then society would be asked to accept at least part of
the responsibility for that decision. The Chinese policy of 'one child
per family' (and its accompanying propaganda about the glories of

childlessness) currently raises a social morality to a particularly advanced form: any individual decision to bear a child affects, it is argued, all other members of the society, and must therefore be considered in social, much more than individual, terms.

On a continuum between an individualistic and a social morality, de Beauvoir and the Chinese family policy stand at opposite poles. But that example serves to illustrate the point about the complexities for feminists and socialists of developing a moral code that is neither potentially socially oppressive through its libertarianism nor socially repressive through its authoritarianism. Many writers other than de Beauvoir have wrestled with the dilemma of developing a morality that in allowing individual choice does not, by the same tolerance, limit it. For socialists the dilemma is perhaps particularly acute since an awareness of the social evils of unrestricted choice is difficult to reconcile with the possibility of extensive personal freedom. And it was on precisely this point that Sartre and de Beauvoir found that their political sympathies were most severely tested by their commitment to individual freedom. In a succession of uneasy relationships and bitter farewells Sartre and de Beauvoir severed their links with one socialist society after another. Long-time sympathizers with the Soviet Union, they had to abandon their friendly association with that state after the gradual deliberalization that followed the uneasy flowering of intellectual diversity in the Khrushchev era after the Twentieth Party Congress. Similarly, Sartre and de Beauvoir gave their support to Castro and the revolution in Cuba. Again, they relinquished that amicable relationship when they learned of Castro's less than entirely liberal policies towards sexual and intellectual minorities. De Beauvoir's *All Said and Done* documents the great sorrow she and Sartre felt for those much loved countries which had seemed to promise the possibility of libertarian socialism. She wrote in 1971 of the Soviet Union:

'The Russians have finally disappointed all our hopes. Never has the situation of the intellectuals been so critical. None of our friends can obtain permission to come and see us any more, and we know that they all feel completely powerless. Amalric, for having told the truth about his country, has once again been sent to Siberia, and there he is dying. The Leningrad trial has clearly shown the anti-semitism that is so rife at government level in the USSR. Not without regret, I believe I shall never see Moscow again.'

(ASD, 364)

Thus the Soviet Union and Cuba join the list of countries which have, in their different ways, betrayed what de Beauvoir regards as central values and standards. The list is extensive and began in the late 1940s with the United States: as described in *The Prime of Life* it was towards the United States that de Beauvoir and Sartre looked in their youth and early maturity for that vitality and exuberance that they found lacking in Europe at the time. Sartre, the first to visit the States, came back amazed and disillusioned: 'they have no sense of tragedy' he remarked to de Beauvoir on his return about the North Americans. Nevertheless the sheer wealth and riches of the United States had amazed Sartre as much as any European of his generation: the well-fed, well-clothed, and well-off GI who arrived in Europe in 1944 appeared as incredible to Sartre and de Beauvoir as to any other citizen. But very rapidly the honeymoon and enchantment with the United States ended:

'I was prepared to love America. It was the homeland of capitalism, yes, but it had helped to save Europe from Fascism; the atomic bomb assured it world leadership and freed it from all fear; books written by certain American liberals had convinced me that a large section of the nation had a clear and serene sense of its responsibilities. The reality was a great shock to me. There flourished among almost all the intellectuals, even those who claimed to be of the left, an Americanism worthy of the chauvinism of my father. . . . What I found most disquieting was the inertia of all these people ceaselessly nagged by the wildest propaganda. No one, as far as I know, was talking about the organisation man yet; but that was whom I described in my reports. . . . I was struck by the absence, even among very young boys and girls, of any interior motivation; they were incapable of thinking, of inventing, of imagining, of choosing, of deciding for themselves; this incapacity was expressed by their conformism.'

(FC, 124)

The personal events – the affair with Nelson Algren and its unhappy end – of de Beauvoir's visits to North America are described in *The Mandarins*. In addition, a more extensive account of her travels in the States is given in *America Day by Day*, something of a catalogue of lecture halls, bus journeys, and the great cities of North America. The book contains a particularly striking photograph of de Beauvoir in New York: the serious and slightly fierce beauty of her face is set against the background of Times Square and provides a vivid contrast between two worlds: an intense, emotionally vital human being contrasted with the monolithic concrete of triumphant capitalism. Not, of course, that the United States was, as de Beauvoir described it, 'the homeland of capitalism'; but the scale of the capitalist enterprise was – and is – significantly larger in the United States than in other industrial capitalist societies. Compared to France in 1945, the United States must have appeared as an entirely new world. Indeed, it has been argued that France even in the 1980s remains – compared to some other industrialized societies – an underdeveloped society. R. W. Johnson, writing of France in 1981, suggested that:

'The achievement of French society since the liberation has, indeed, been to combine a series of prodigious social changes – rapid urbanisation, high economic growth and considerable occupational change – with a fundamental and underlying social immobility. . . . It would be difficult to modify very greatly the picture we have already assembled of a rigidly stratified society in which the inequalities between social classes exceed, in almost all respects, those found in virtually any other industrial nation. It is, indeed, some measure of the French situation to say that France is more typical of the semi-developed than the developed world. A search for comparably unequal societies will take one not into the neighbouring countries of northern Europe, but into some of the more brutal and authoritarian states of Latin America.'

(Johnson 1981: 123–24)

This passage is cited to suggest – as much as an argument about French society – a mode of analysis of the social world that is markedly and fundamentally different from that of de Beauvoir, one which highlights some of the intrinsic problems in de Beauvoir's political analysis which lead her to make what are at times highly suspect, because vaguely located and over-generalized, judgements about the social world and social relations. De Beauvoir, in writing about the United States in *America Day by Day* (and almost equally in her study of China, *The Long March*), uses as her material for discussion about a particular society its literature and the opinions of the intelligentsia. Johnson, on the other hand, refers not to expressed opinion or points of view but to empirical evidence about social reality. He does not, therefore, endorse a vague theory about the high form of civilization of the French or other such Francophile beliefs but confronts the material reality of French social and productive relations. De Beauvoir, on the other hand, takes issue with the United States (or China or any other society that comes to her attention) in terms of what that society says about itself, rather than in terms of a dispassionate analysis of the social and economic structure.

But de Beauvoir's eye for social relations never focused in great detail on the workings of a particular society. As already pointed out, she had, and has, a very sharp sense of possible injustice and tyranny, but rather less of an understanding of the day-to-day workings of social life. Indeed, an exaggerated criticism of de Beauvoir's writing on politics and on individual states would be that she represents all the worst excesses of the over-active traveller who visits a society and a culture, takes a set of photographs, and disappears again. In her youth de Beauvoir plunged into travel with the passion of someone who clearly believed that the world contained endless possibility and diversity, and *The Prime of Life* documents her insatiable curiosity about the countries which she visited. The curiosity was never confined to the more pleasant aspects of these countries: she and Sartre, on the travels described in *The Prime of Life* and *Force of Circumstance*, sought out the poorer sections of the cities and towns which they visited. Athens and Naples, for example, are known to them as more than the cities of the Parthenon and the view of the Bay of Naples, they are also seen as cities of disease, overcrowding, and beggary. Thus de Beauvoir writes on Naples:

'We felt something of Naples's frightfulness – the naked scabby infants; the scrofulous and the crippled; the open, purulent sores and the livid, abscess like faces; not to mention insanitary slum apartments (with bills posted on them that said either CONDEMNED or UNFIT FOR HUMAN OCCUPATION) where innumerable families swarmed. Blows were exchanged over cabbage stalks or bits of rotten meat picked up in the gutter, while at every street corner stood a smiling, beatific image of the Virgin Mary, adorned with gilded drapery and surrounded by flowers and guttering candles.'

(PL, 267)

But, she continues, she and Sartre could always escape from these conditions. Accessible to them were the more pleasant districts of Naples, and whatever physical hardships they both experienced were essentially temporary and subject to their control. As Orwell was to remark in *The Road to Wigan Pier* of his own experience of poverty, middle-class people can always buy themselves out of poverty and, more important still perhaps for the difference it makes in their understanding of the social world, exercise a degree of control over the conditions and circumstances of their existence that is denied to the poor. Thus the sense of freedom and the very notion of personal choice and personal definition that form so important a part of de Beauvoir's view of the world do not spring from nowhere; they have a material basis and a location in the degree to which individuals are free from want and disease. Unlike many individuals of her class de Beauvoir recognized and acknowledged poverty, but what is missing from this understanding is a perception of the ways in which poverty and material hardship structure social relations and social life. Crucially, what is created is an endless calculation about every aspect of social life, a calculation which is essentially concerned with the material implications of actions and choices. And in any society in which material inequalities exist, the possibility of poverty creates even among those who are not poor a fear of the consequences of poverty that in its turn creates avarice, greed, or fear. So it is not simply the poor who suffer poverty, it is also those who might be plunged into its abyss.

Given the circumstances of de Beauvoir's childhood and adolescence – particularly the impoverishment of her family after the First World War – it is strange that de Beauvoir did not consider a little more fully the implications for individuals of both their actual or their possible wealth and poverty. It is not that she does not acknowledge poverty, it is that she excludes from her consideration of the motivations of individuals their calculations about material life. For example, in her novels economic constraints never affect the actions of the characters: women do not stay with men because of material necessity, nor are they attracted to men because of the material rewards and possibilities that men might offer. All is emotional need and emotional choice, powerful motivations in themselves but motivations and needs that do not exist in a vague, abstract space. On the contrary, the constant, shared needs of all human beings take on different forms in different societies and are given diverse meanings by diverse social structures. It is thus the interplay of forces that is missing in de Beauvoir's work: the factors are there, the poverty, the deprivation, the sense of human need for affection and intimacy, but they are located singly and in isolation rather than collectively and in dialectical relationship the one to another.

Overall, then, when de Beauvoir discovers a category – be it man or woman or old age – she will explore very fully all the possibilities of that category, but what she will not do is explore the emergence of that category as a result of the interaction of various social forces and social structures. This limitation of her model of the social world has already been discussed in relation to her study of women. In relation to her discussion of politics, many readers of *The Long March* or *America Day by Day* will be dissatisfied by the mixture of somewhat simple interpretation

112   SIMONE DE BEAUVOIR

and official propaganda that these works contain. (It is interesting to note here that in *All Said and Done* de Beauvoir remarks that one country in the world – namely India – simply escapes her understanding. Faced with the complexities of Indian society and culture de Beauvoir metaphorically throws up her hands and leaves understanding and analysis to other pens.) Equally, many readers will be disappointed by the massive work which de Beauvoir produced on old age. In over six hundred pages of text de Beauvoir produces a great deal of everything that has ever been written in the west on the subject of ageing. The approach to the subject is similar to that used in *The Second Sex*: a first section on biology ('The physiological characteristic of ageing in man is what Dr. Destrem calls an "unfavourable transformation of the tissues"' (OA, 30)), followed by a review of ageing in a number of non-industrial and 'historical' societies, followed by interpretations of ageing in works of largely western literature. The order is, therefore, identical: biology, followed by illustration from diverse societies and from literature. The underprivileged group is again interpreted as 'the other': as women are to men in *The Second Sex*, the aged appear in *Old Age* as 'the other' to the young. The difference between the two books is that by the time she came to write *Old Age* de Beauvoir had discovered the importance of material life, and *Old Age* is therefore liberally sprinkled with references to the poverty of the elderly in industrial capitalism. Yet this discovery leads de Beauvoir to an overemphasis on the material world that is as problematic as her earlier idealism: having discovered the concepts of alienation and the exploitation of labour de Beauvoir then introduces them as concepts capable of wholesale explanation. Thus she is able to write, in the Conclusion to *Old Age*:

> 'What should a society be, so that in his last years a man might still be a man? The answer is simple: he would always have to have been treated as a man. . . . Old age exposes the failure of our entire civilisation. It is the whole man that must be re-made, it is the whole relationship between man and man that must be recast if we wish the old person's state to be acceptable. . . . Society cares about the individual only in so far as he is profitable.'
> (OA, 603–04)

A harsh indictment, and one that might also be applied to western society's treatment of the disabled or the mentally ill. But de Beauvoir's discovery of materialist analysis leads her to explain everything about the condition of the old in industrial capitalism in terms of the relationship of the aged worker to the labour process.

Now it is certainly the case that industrial capitalism does not provide extensively for the aged. On the other hand it does make a minimal provision, whereas according to the strict and absolute logic that de Beauvoir ascribes to capitalism it should provide nothing and cast aside with a complete, callous disregard those least able, or unable, to contribute to the accumulation of profit. But although hardly a caring social system, within capitalism other, more humanitarian values coexist with the profit motive. The early years of industrialization in the capitalist west were certainly marked by ruthless exploitation but the history of social reform in every industrialized society bears witness to the possibility of the development within capitalism of those values and standards which contribute a fundamental challenge to the profit motive. The motives of social reformers were often mixed (for example, Jane Humphries has outlined the sexist assumptions underlying early protective legislation about the employment of women in Great Britain) but they all shared a concern with the conditions in which people lived and worked, and which were, in their view, an affront to human dignity.

Thus what emerges from a study of social reform in the west is a mixture of motives and interests within one social system. Bourgeois society may be capable of endorsing wholesale exploitation but it is equally capable of encouraging and allowing movements of social reform and liberalization. Crude interpretations of capitalism and bourgeois society tend to obscure the complexities of these divergent strands within one social formation; what they certainly omit altogether is any discussion of the progressive nature of changes and developments that have taken place within western capitalism in the last three hundred years. It was, for example, bourgeois men who, in England in the seventeenth century, championed and articulated the cause of representative democracy; equally it was the same group who in the eighteenth century established fundamental concepts about the rule of law and the equality of citizens before the law. As E. P. Thompson wrote in *Whigs and Hunters*:

'The law, in its forms and traditions, entailed principles of equity and universality which, perforce, had to be extended to all sorts and degrees of men. . . . The rhetoric and the rules of a society are something a great deal more than sham. In the same moment they may modify, in profound ways, the behaviour of the powerful, and mystify the powerless. They may disguise the true realities of power, but, at the same time, they may curb that power and check its intrusions.'

(Thompson 1977: 264–65)

And Thompson continues, 'We reach, then, not a simple conclusion (law = class power) but a complex contradictory one.'

It is not a sentence which could easily be applied to any of de Beauvoir's works. With the possible exception of *A Very Easy Death* her work does not offer much suggestion of the complexities of human action and motivation. *The Second Sex* is organized around a rigid polarity and dichotomy between men and women, *Old Age* juxtaposes with the same rigidity the old and industrial capitalism, the travel books condemn wholeheartedly or praise with unqualified enthusiasm, and the sheer scale of the autobiography suggests an attitude to experience that is documentary rather than interpretative. Throughout this substantial body of work de Beauvoir remains consistent to principles of honesty, integrity, and a concern for human beings. Equally, she offers a mode of analysis which can over-simplify complex issues, and suggests a deceptive and perhaps dangerous simplicity in the answers to social and personal problems.

In order to locate the reasons for the difficulties inherent in de Beauvoir's interpretation of the social world, it is necessary to return to *The Second Sex*, and to note in particular the rejection in that work by de Beauvoir of Freud and Marx. Freud is rejected because of de Beauvoir's refusal to accept his concept of the unconscious; Engels and, by implication, Marx are rejected because of what de Beauvoir describes as their 'economic monism' (SS, 54). Both readings – of Freud and Marx – deny the complexities of the work of both men: of Freud's discussion of the diverse elements that go into the construction of human emotional and sexual identity, and of Marx's constant reiteration of the need to understand the contradictions and the diversity of all human societies. It can be allowed that it would have been difficult for de Beauvoir to read, in the late 1940s, much of the work of either Freud or Marx since it was not until the 1960s that extensive translations of the work of both appeared in France. But even if *The Second Sex* does belong to an era which knew little of Freud or Marx, this is insufficient reason to explain some of the limits of de Beauvoir's later work.

But Freud and Marx have a further importance in the context of a discussion of de Beauvoir's work, beyond their possible impact on her. It is that the work of both men represents a highly developed form of analysis and rational thought. While neither man lost sight of what they regarded as fundamental organizing principles in human activity they nevertheless allowed that human beings and human societies did not, and do not, proceed along straightforward, simple paths. Furthermore, both regarded choice as something undertaken in complex and perhaps confusing situations; neither supposed that adult human beings could choose between simple, clearly differentiated possibilities. So to regard – as some feminists have done – the work of de Beauvoir as representing all that is most rigid, most representative of 'male' thought, is to misrepresent the work of many men, and to fail to perceive that the excessive order and occasional rigidity of de Beauvoir are derived from sources that have also produced work of great sophistication and complexity. To condemn de Beauvoir as 'phallo-centric' or her work as 'male' is appropriate only if all male thought is as rigidly structured and didactic as de Beauvoir herself can be. More important, the issue of whether or not de Beauvoir is a 'male' writer raises the question of whether it is appropriate to label the work of any writer as demonstrating certain sexual characteristics. If de Beauvoir is defined as a 'male' writer, then the next question to consider is whether what she says should be disallowed and dismissed because of how she says it.

Thus attempting to define de Beauvoir's writing in terms of the supposed intellectual character of one sex or the other immediately raises questions about the 'essential' characteristics of either sex. If it is argued that – for whatever reason – men and women tend to write in different ways (men more logically and women more diffusely, for example), then de Beauvoir's work and analysis could be said to unite some of the more negative characteristics of both sexes, and to personify the limitations that are produced in either sex through the workings of an educational and cultural system that dichotomizes both the experiences and the articulation of experience of both men and women. In terms of de Beauvoir's own biography she herself admits that she identified her mother with 'feminine' chaos and subjectivity, and her father with 'masculine' order and logic. The attraction of higher education, of Sartre, and of intellectual life was that they all offered a way out of what appeared as confused, incoherent, petit-bourgeois life, and the life within that social stratum of a wife and mother. So the work that emerged from this impetus towards a certain kind of order was structured by a personal motive to order and categorize social life and interpersonal relations. The style of the novels in particular has this didactic quality: like Victorian moral tales, they are organized around the demonstration of the pitfalls in certain paths of action.

So in all de Beauvoir's work there emerges a consistent motive towards order and coherence, towards the solution of human problems by 'correct' actions. Thus throughout de Beauvoir's work there is a constant identification by the author with culture, in the sense that she identifies with the moral systems and culturally specific difficulties of the individuals she is writing about rather than with the particular individual characteristics of a set of personal dilemmas. The line in literature – and literary criticism – between the social character and the individual character is a thin one: for some authors and critics, all is social, for others all is individual. De Beauvoir's characters tend to fall into the first camp: they represent, in a way which the created characters of Eliot, Tolstoy, or Austen do not, social problems. That is not to say that the problems which beset men and women are not (in a variety of ways and to different degrees) social in origin, but that individuals – because of their diverse biographies and temperaments – interact with their social environment in different ways. For example, although some married bourgeois women in pre-revolutionary Russia may have taken lovers, it was not every married woman whose love for a man other than her husband led her to a tragic death. So the fact of an illicit passion, which others shared with Anna Karenina, did not – because of the different psychological characteristics of those others –necessarily lead them to the same end. But the possibilities of different outcomes for different people in the same circumstances is not explored by de Beauvoir: the same situation (most typically the overvaluation by women of their emotional relationship with a man) leads to the same conclusion. Inevitable, for those feminists convinced that women are always the victims in heterosexual relationships, de Beauvoir's fiction provides excellent material. Here, after all, is the *grande dame* of twentieth-century feminism demonstrating exactly how inevitably doomed are relationships between men and women that involve the passions or what de Beauvoir might see as 'nature'.

So 'nature' (emotional life, sexual passion, the feelings that are sometimes legitimated or explained as 'love') is to be ordered in de Beauvoir's fiction. The novels are not, therefore, a discussion of the ambiguities of human actions and needs, but a search for, and a statement of, moral clarity. The author identifies – to put it in Freudian terms – more or less exclusively with the super-ego, at the expense of the id. Or to put it another way, there is a determination on de Beauvoir's part to establish herself as a strong presence in the novels. She is not an author who views her characters from a distance; the characters are ciphers of the author's motives, the means by which de Beauvoir establishes herself as a positive presence, since her characters, in their limited appearance as human beings, allow her to impose on them the problems which she perceives in adult emotional relationships. Thus the characters are, in a sense, helpless before the will of the author; their lack of created character and personality makes them deeply pervious to the intentions of the author. De Beauvoir is not alone, of course, in writing literature that is concerned essentially with morality: moral concerns are the central pivot of most European fiction. What distinguishes de Beauvoir's use of fiction is not, therefore, its part in the discussion of morality, but the projection of de Beauvoir's own experiences and dilemmas on to the fictional lives of her characters.

Again, it must be said that in writing about the familiar, de Beauvoir does exactly what countless other authors have done. But the difference between her and other authors is that in her attempt to abandon subjectivity and avoid writing fictionalized autobiography she creates characters who are largely drained of psychological characteristics. In de Beauvoir's very earliest published fiction (the collection of short stories published under the title *When Things of the Spirit Come First*) it is clear that she has been unable to divorce herself from the characters that she has created. She admits in the Preface to the English translation that the stories were deliberately designed to expose 'some of the defects' of the world which she knew. This motive was to continue in the later fiction, but *When Things of the Spirit Come First* is an interesting collection in that it demonstrates de Beauvoir in her least distanced and most autobiographical mode. The predominant characteristics of this mode are, first, the belief that characters are straightforwardly formed by social pressures, rather than by a combination of personal and social circumstances. The second is the presentation of heterosexuality in terms of passive women and active men. Although female characters in de Beauvoir's later novels do come to develop a degree of independent sexuality and sexual desire, they all share the ability of Marcelle in *When Things of the Spirit Come First* to overlook the moral failings of their male partners, or the difficulties of a particular relationship, once in the arms of the beloved. Or, as de Beauvoir describes it:

'It was only at night, when he took her in his arms, that Marcell's faith in him and in his love came back: to see this child she watched over like a mother during the day change into an imperious young male overwhelmed her and she yielded to his whims with intense pleasure.'

(WTS, 36)

The model of sexuality is one, therefore, that contemporary feminists have come to regard with suspicion: the dichotomization of male and female desire, the glorification of heterosexual intercourse as a panacea for emotional and social difficulties, and the construction of sexuality largely in terms of genital sexuality. The social construction of sexual desire, or even the absence of sexual intercourse in relationships deeply imbued with sexual passion and feeling, are not possibilities allowed in de Beauvoir's fiction. Again, to cite contrasting examples in the work of another writer. George Eliot, in describing Dorothea's disappointments on her honeymoon with Casaubon, in *Middlemarch*, did so in terms of metaphor – Dorothea sits and cries amongst the ruins of ancient Rome. She sobs, we might conclude, not just for the failure of Casaubon's potency, but for her own dreams of the possibility that men, and male order and sexuality, could render the world intelligible and credible. Equally, we do not need to be told in *Daniel Deronda* that the relationship between Deronda and Gwendolen Harleth, although never physically consummated, is deeply charged with sexual passion. That Eliot does not consummate this relationship between these characters is a feature of her skill and sophistication as a novelist: she tells us instead to consider the varieties and possibilities of sexual relations and the way in which women's desire for men constructs the very power and strength that men may, or may not, then use as a weapon over women. Deronda does not need a sexual relationship with Gwendolen because he can communicate to her by other means those ways of living which, we are led to believe, might constitute Gwendolen's ultimate moral salvation.

But much of the possible richness and diversity of the emotional and sexual worlds of men and women is absent from de Beauvoir. Friendship, motherhood, fatherhood also join the list of absences in the novels. It is true that in her autobiography de Beauvoir includes many friends as important people in her life, but the nature of these friendships is often presented in unambiguously straightforward terms. De Beauvoir does not, for example, consider exactly why she needs the company of the young student Sylvie le Bon whom she describes in *All Said and Done*: she admits that Sylvie reminds her of herself when young, but that admission might have been followed by reflections on why an individual chooses people who re-create his or her own problems, or on the narcissism involved in the choice as a friend of a person young enough to be guided and perhaps moulded. To take the issue even further, there is surely a possibility that choosing as a friend someone younger and yet similar amounts to finding a way of satisfying needs for corroboration and clarification. Equally, it is not unlikely that de Beauvoir was gratified in this particular friendship by the possibility of nurturing another human being. Sartre had provided endless opportunities for the expression of this need, but the claims of that relationship were both more extensive and more limited than those of the friendship with Sylvie.

Throughout de Beauvoir's work there is, therefore, an enormous moral force and concern that is coupled with a singular absence of perceptions of the ambiguities and complexities of the human state. Social life is a matter of x causing y, sexuality is always phallic and never diffuse, and emotional life is a dangerous matter unless brought under constant, rigorous, rational control. De Beauvoir's solutions to the difficulties, injustices, and problems that she perceives in the world – be they personal or social – therefore follow her analysis in its essential simplicity. She is absolutely right and valiant in her attack on injustice and poverty, but limited in the solutions that she would propose to these problems, since the rigidity and prescriptive nature of many of her solutions might well create further problems. So it is with her analysis of human difficulties: she demands the rejection, through choice, of emotionally complex or problematic situations but overlooks the existence in all human beings of needs and desires – for example both for independence and dependence – that are frequently contradictory, not least in terms of their results in human actions. De Beauvoir's consistent call for female economic and emotional independence and autonomy is but one example of her partial consideration of the needs of women. Certainly, all human beings need to be able to act, and choose, in conditions (both material and emotional) that are free from constraint and coercion; yet at the same time as a need for independence exists, so too might a need for intimacy and continuity. Many of these needs are – as de Beauvoir rightly points out – currently distorted and denied in bourgeois society. Nevertheless, in proposing and outlining alternatives de Beauvoir rather too rapidly and comprehensively rejects those possibilities within bourgeois society which have – as a result of human activity and struggle – produced the conditions of a genuine emancipation. In doing so, she provides a model of the social world, as black or white, good or bad, which lends itself to the politics of rejection or acceptance – in the context of feminism those analyses of sexual relations which divide the world, at all times and for all purposes, into two opposing and quite distinct sexes.

6
_____Conclusion_____

Nowhere are the contradictions of de Beauvoir's work better expressed than by the author herself, in an interview with Alice Jardine published in 1979. Discussing the possibility of the existence of differences between men and women in terms of the way the two sexes express themselves through language, de Beauvoir says: 'I consider it almost antifeminist to say that there is a feminine nature which expresses itself differently, that a woman speaks her body more than a man, because after all, men also speak their bodies when they write' (Jardine 1979: 230). Three pages later, de Beauvoir remarks that Virginia Woolf's writing was:

'In the best sense of the word . . . very feminine, and by that I mean that women are supposed to be very sensitive . . . I don't know . . . to all the sensations of nature, much more so than men, much more contemplative. . . . It's this quality that marks her best works. Colette is another case in point. Even if they had not wanted to make their writing feminine, it is nevertheless very feminine.'

(Jardine 1979: 233)

On the one hand denying the existence of essential female character-istics ('women are made not born') and yet on the other suggesting that women are in some sense the more sensitive sex, de Beauvoir poses for all critics – be they feminist or not – difficult problems of definition. That she is a feminist is an unquestioned assumption of feminist writing, yet like all such assumptions there are major problems about this uncritical acceptance of de Beauvoir's place within feminism. Not the least of the problems is that of exactly how feminism is deemed to be constituted, should de Beauvoir be considered as a feminist *par excellence*. That issue – of the relationship between de Beauvoir and feminism – will be explained shortly. But first, some review of critical discussions of de Beauvoir is necessary.

Given the extent of de Beauvoir's work and the attention that it has attracted, it might be expected that critics and defenders would be numerous. However, the secondary literature on de Beauvoir is both limited and curiously muted in its criticism.[1] For feminist critics, this could be explained by an unwillingness to challenge or criticize the work of a woman who has contributed an enormous amount to the development of feminism. But others besides feminists have been equally unforthcoming in their discussion of de Beauvoir. Part of this lack of interest can be explained by the traditional sexism of many academics and literary critics: because de Beauvoir has written (although by no means exclusively) about women it is quite acceptable to dismiss her work as 'merely' about women. Women, and women who write about women, are easy to dismiss as outside the considera-tion of a serious-minded critic. That this view confirms all that de Beauvoir ever said about women's existence as the 'second sex' is of course of no interest whatsoever to those who see women as in some sense outside the main concerns of the serious, male world. Thus when traditional critics have discussed de Beauvoir's work they have seen it either in the standard terms of literary criticism or as an interesting addition to the truly substantial work of Sartre. It is, as this essay has demonstrated, impossible to write about de Beauvoir without also writing about Sartre: the problem lies in the conception of the nature of the relationship, and the stress placed on the contribution of each to the other's work and to intellectual life in general. For some male critics the illict nature of the relationship (which in the 1980s seems quietly domestic in its essential ingredients) provokes severe, moralistic condemnation. Thus, for example, C. B. Radford wrote in 1965 of de Beauvoir: 'It is a pity that her laudable criticism of dishonesty should lead her to exhibitionism and excesses in personal behaviour' (Radford 1965: 103). And Maurice Cranston, in 1978, dismissed de Beauvoir's credentials for writing about women by saying that: 'Unmarried, and uninterested in motherhood, living in fact, to all intents and purposes just like a man, Simone de Beauvoir is not ideally qualified by experience to write the kind of book she hoped to write' (Cranston 1978: 181).

Both comments, of course, will illustrate to feminists the well-known perversity of sexism: that women are never supposed to be anything except orthodox and conservative, and that unlike men their qualifications for any task must always be immaculate. De Beauvoir is thus disqualified from writing about motherhood by her childlessness, and barred from a place in the serious political world by the unconventionality of her private world – an unconventionality which, in a male intellectual, would probably not provoke a single remark. The same kind of double standard permeates discussion of the contribution of both Sartre and de Beauvoir to philosophy: Sartre is the major intellectual force, de Beauvoir the illustrative footnote. And the sexism here is twofold: first, the obvious assumption that a man's work will automatically be of higher value than that of a woman, and the second, more subtle assumption, that identifies only the author of a work and never those who have contributed in other ways. Obviously, Sartre wrote the books and pamphlets for which he is world famous, but equally obviously (and by Sartre's own admission) those works were formed and much enhanced by the hours that he spent in conversation with de Beauvoir, who provided that invaluable, and hardly untypical, female service of an audience for a busy and preoccupied man. De Beauvoir does not appear as the wife 'without whom this book would never have been written' and did not undertake the usual domestic services that are assumed in such acknowledgements, but on the other hand she was a constantly available source of criticism and validation for Sartre. As he was to write, in a letter to de Beauvoir: 'you are the armour of my life, my conscience and my reason. All that I have done of value has been because of you.'[2]

Nevertheless, the relationship remains charged with ambiguities, not least the possible one-sidedness of the contribution made by the one to the other – in this case the greater contribution being made by de Beauvoir. It was de Beauvoir who scoured Paris for food during the occupation, de Beauvoir who listened to Sartre's emotional problems, de Beauvoir who read Sartre's work, and who, above all else, provided an absolute consistency and continuity in Sartre's life. If Sartre, at the beginning of the relationship, had given de Beauvoir the confidence to escape from the prison of her petit-bourgeois world and encouraged her to write, then he was richly repaid in the later rewards of the relationship. De Beauvoir's perception of her debt of gratitude to Sartre has led one critic to mock the relationship: in a review of Carol Ascher's *Simone de Beauvoir: A Life of Freedom*, Angela Carter wrote:

'We know she was almost as clever as he was because, at that time, de Beauvoir still thought it worthwhile to tell the world via the autobiographical details on her back flaps that she had come second to Sartre in their university finals. And, goodness me, wasn't coming second to Jean-Paul Sartre – Jean-Paul Sartre! – something to be proud of?'

(Carter 1982: 156)

and she continues:

'Yet what, one wonders, would have been the intellectual history of 20th century Europe had de Beauvoir somehow managed to scrape together that handful of extra marks and pip Sartre at the post? What might de Beauvoir not have done had it been objectively proved to her that she was cleverer than Sartre?'

(Carter 1982: 157)

In this mockery of de Beauvoir's description of herself as someone who came 'second to Jean-Paul Sartre', there is an important point: de Beauvoir's emphasis, at least in her youth and early maturity, on intelligence, and on intelligence that was approved, constructed, and sanctioned by institutions dominated by men and organized around a particular kind of bourgeois, competitive notion of 'intelligence'. However, to identify the teaching of the Sorbonne in 1929 (or even in the 1980s) simply as patriarchal and bourgeois is to overlook and disallow those academic ideals of critical inquiry which, however badly served by the institutions of higher education, nevertheless inspired the work of de Beauvoir.

So the interrelationship of class and gender factors in the formation of the thought of de Beauvoir is complex, and both factors are further complicated by biographical circumstances. Brought up in a home which epitomized a disjunction between characteristics traditionally associated with men (rationality, scepticism, anti-clericalism, active sexuality, freedom of movement) and those associated with women (passivity, silent suffering, superstitious religious beliefs, and conventional sexuality), de Beauvoir sought escape from the fate of petit-bourgeois women of her time through the characteristics of her father rather than her mother. The very dichotomy of her parents' major and salient personal characteristics – and the perception in her adolescence of the superiority of her father's life to that of her mother – encouraged de Beauvoir to see the characteristics of her father as liberating. Certainly, in this she was largely correct: rationality and rational thought are means through which individuals can acquire the ability to control their fate, and are infinitely preferable to the narrow beliefs and rigid views of religious observance and narrow chauvinism, be it class or culture based.

But the problem in de Beauvoir's work, and in the view of the world that she suggests to her readers, is not that of naming the conditions women should be liberated from (that is quite unambiguous), but of where this liberation should take both them and men. De Beauvoir represents all that is best in feminism (and indeed it must be said in western liberalism) in her constant, unequivocal support for women's rights to education, employment, and the means of controlling their fertility. At the same time, she represents much that is limited about western feminism – and again, western liberalism – in that she asks few questions about differences, particularly inequalities of class and race, between women. De Beauvoir's analysis of women's condition – and her suggestions for its improvement – can therefore lead to two possible developments: first, to improvements in the situation of women which neither threaten established, and often male, interests, nor remove the very conditions in the social world which create inequality; second, to the reproduction by women, through an essentially bourgeois emancipation, of much that de Beauvoir finds least acceptable in western, bourgeois society: namely, individualism, competitiveness, and an endorsement of a hierarchical social world. Now these factors, and the success of an individual though them, may lead to the competence and self-confidence necessary to write *The Second Sex*, but they are just as likely to lead to the other – unacceptable – face of bourgeois society and western capitalism. So in de Beauvoir's call to women to reject their secondary status lie not only the seeds of women's liberation and emancipation from existing society but also the seeds of a form of liberation and emancipation that lead to a closer identification with it. Indeed, in a particularly perceptive essay on de Beauvoir Margaret Walters has suggested that de Beauvoir's

'emancipated woman sounds just like that familiar nineteenth-century character, the self-made man. (And isn't that the model underlying all her philosophic sophistication?) Early capitalist man, dominating and exploiting the natural world, living to produce, viewing his own life as a product shaped by will, and suppressing those elements in himself – irrationality, sexuality – that might reduce his normal and economic efficiency. His moral and emotional life is seen in capitalist terms – as de Beauvoir tends to see hers.'

(Walters 1976: 357)

The only ways in which de Beauvoir could ensure that women's emancipation would lead to a major change, and improvement, in the social world would be either to identify women, as women, with all that is careful, nurturing, unaggressive, and peaceful, or to establish a link between feminism and socialism of such a kind that it would be impossible for one woman's emancipation to be achieved at the cost of another's. De Beauvoir opts for neither of these possibilities: although a life-long socialist she does not establish in her analysis of the situation of women those links between patriarchy and capitalism which have now been widely discussed. De Beauvoir admitted in 1977 that in 1949 she assumed that 'socialism would lead to the emancipation of women', but by the 1970s she had come to the conclusion that this would not be the case. She thus argued for a women's movement, 'independent of the class struggle', which, if successful, would 'shake society' (Jardine 1979: 235)

So de Beauvoir does espouse the view, commonplace among feminists be they socialist, Marxist, or radical, that a reorganization of the sexual division of labour would bring about fundamental changes in industrial capitalism. Nancy Chodorow and Michele Barrett, to use but two examples, have both argued that a feminist revolution would produce a qualitatively and structurally different form of society. Thus Chodorow, in *The Reproduction of Mothering*, suggests that if men learned to acquire more expressive and nurturing characteristics, then:

'This would reduce men's needs to guard their masculinity and their control of social and cultural spheres which treat and define women as secondary and powerless, and would help women to develop the autonomy which too much embeddedness in relationships has often taken from them.'

(Chodorow 1978: 218)

The consequence of the development of a more equal distribution between the sexes of the responsibilities for nurturing would be a change in men's attitude to the major issues of the social world: the argument is that the nurturing role creates in individuals a concern for others that will manifest itself in care for individuals on a community scale. Barrett's argument, in *Women's Oppression Today*, is much more firmly located in a materialist analysis of western society; in her conclusion she suggests that:

> 'The liberation of women would require, first, a redivision of the labour and responsibilities of childcare. Whether privatised or collectivised, it would be mandatory that this be shared between men and women. Second, the actual or assumed dependence of women on a male wage (or capital) would need to be done away with. Third, the ideology of gender would need to be transformed. *None of these seem to me to be compatible with capitalism as it exists in Britain and comparable societies today.*'
>
> (Barrett 1980: 254)

The italics are mine, and used to emphasize the point that Barrett is making, and its similarity to the position of de Beauvoir and Chodorow. All three authors accept, and argue, that a transformation in gender relations and in the sexual division of labour would have a transforming effect on society as we now know it in the west. What is at stake here is not whether or not alterations in the sexual division of labour would produce differences in social organization; obviously alterations in child-care responsibilities and the ending of the absolute identification of women with the care of children would produce a society different in some, albeit important, respects from the one in which we now live. But it is quite another matter to believe that the new, reordered society in which both men and women care for children would be non-capitalist and therefore essentially and fundamentally different from contemporary western society. It is not inconceivable that the mandatory sharing of child care suggested by Barrett, and the sharing of nurturing advocated by Chodorow, could be integrated into advanced capitalism and offer no significant threat to that system's organizing principle of the extraction of surplus value from labour for private profit. Indeed, when Barrett writes of child care 'whether privatised or collectivised' she opens up vistas of privately run nurseries and day-care centres which are as perfectly compatible with capitalism as private schools.

Barrett's analysis has recently been discussed at some length by Johanna Brenner and Maria Ramas, and their criticisms of *Women's Oppression Today* have touched on an issue that is equally relevant to de Beauvoir. Brenner and Ramas, in suggesting problems in *Women's Oppression Today*, argue that many socialist feminists, 'Barrett among them, are extremely reluctant to acknowledge any role for biological differences in determining women's social position. Underlying this reluctance is a healthy concern that any such focus may inadvertently lead down the path to biological determinism' (Brenner and Ramas 1984: 47).

Indeed, a discussion of biological differences has often been ruled out of order by feminists – with particular vehemence in the case of the feminist rejection of Freud – because of the awful possibility of the construction of any argument that might seem to justify the status quo.[3] And de Beauvoir stands very firmly within that tradition – her emphasis on the cultural construction of femininity goes very far towards a denial of the female body, except in so far as it can be a vehicle for heterosexual transcendence. As Adrienne Rich has written:

> 'Patriarchal thought has united female biology to its own narrow specifications. The feminist vision has recoiled from female biology for these reasons; it will, I believe, come to view our physicality as a resource, rather than a destiny. . . . The ancient, continuing envy, awe, and dread of the male for the female capacity to create life has repeatedly taken the form of hatred for every other female aspect of creativity. . . . No wonder that many intellectual and creative women have insisted that they were "human beings" first and women only incidentally, have minimised their physicality and their bonds with other women. The body has been made so problematic for women that it has often seemed easier to shrug it off and travel as a disembodied spirit.'
>
> (Rich 1979: 40)

The passage was not written with de Beauvoir as an explicit focus, yet it is a perfectly appropriate comment on de Beauvoir's own relationship with both an individual and a collective female biology, and on her part in establishing a feminist tradition that sought, in intellectual pursuits, systems, and activities largely dominated by men, an escape from the world constructed around the fulfilment of a female biology.

The narrowness, the constraint, and the dependence of the domestic world of women were, and are, such that de Beauvoir's arguments still have a considerable resonance. But what also has to be considered is the nature, and the value, of the emancipation that de Beauvoir wishes for women. Independence and autonomy are values deeply embedded within capitalism itself (self-reliance, autonomy, self-help, standing-on-your-feet are the essential characteristics of every Anglo-Saxon hero on a scale that stretches from Robinson Crusoe to the owner of a mortgaged semi-detached house) and in seeking to extend the ownership of both material and cultural capital from men to women de

Beauvoir endorses values derived from the capitalist ethic of individual responsibility.

But while politically quite out of sympathy with the right, de Beauvoir very fully represents many of the contradictions and the ambiguities of western feminism. On two major issues in particular – the relationship of women to their biology and the concept of women's emancipation and/or liberation in a hierarchical, capitalist society – she epitomizes all that can produce divisions within feminism. De Beauvoir's uneasy relationship with female biology remains characteristic of feminism: on the one hand there is a tendency towards emotional and physical androgyny (so that women's capacity for motherhood becomes a fact that can be organized by co-parenting and day-care centres and not that more complex set of needs and desires, of both men and women, recognized by Freud) and on the other an assertion of femininity that amounts to a glorification of any instance of human biology that is specifically female. Equally, de Beauvoir's call for the economic independence of women overlooks the problems of divisions and hierarchies between wage labourers and the many different interests that women may have within occupational structures – both for themselves and for their related others. It is thus not surprising that de Beauvoir becomes the 'free' woman for many feminists in the United States: she provides an explanation, and endorsement, of the economically self-sufficient heterosexual woman with liberal sympathies which is perfectly in accord with the values of North American liberalism.[4]

Yet for socialist or radical feminists, de Beauvoir, for all her strengths and courage, remains problematic. For radical feminists she fails to offer a full assertion of femininity: motherhood *per se* is not praised, sexuality is essentially organized as heterosexuality, and de Beauvoir explicitly rejects those claims – by women in France and elsewhere – that women have been forced by men to express themselves, in terms of both language and the symbolic structures of thought, in patriarchal forms and systems. For socialist feminists de Beauvoir provides little assistance in the solution of that essential and crucial (if intractable) problem of the relationship between patriarchy and capitalism. De Beauvoir finds patriarchy in all societies, be they capitalist or feudal, and her accounts of social life invariably minimize the differences both within, and between, social formations. It is not, perhaps, simply a further example of that obsession with empirical evidence and hostility to theory that has been deemed typical of the Anglo-Saxon intellectual tradition to suggest that de Beauvoir's grand theory – combining as it does a belief in a universal, and apparently undifferentiated, capacity for choice and a model of sexual relations that dichotomizes men and women, and makes of men universal oppressors – combines some of the more misleading, and dangerous, values of the west: namely an idealistic belief in human freedom that is constructed independently of any consideration of constraint, and a naturalistic differentiation of the sexes that limits the freedom of both sexes to establish identities that are biologically based but not biologically determined, and at the same time allows the organization by the state of rigidly structured sex-appropriate behaviour. Certainly de Beauvoir wishes women to be freed of the constraints of traditional femininity but what she offers in its place suggests many of the worst excesses of western patriarchal ideology – a belief in the value of emotional independence rather than of integrated and co-operative interdependence, and a model of sexuality that has little place for anything except highly individualized heterosexuality.

Despite these criticisms and comments this discussion of de Beauvoir must end on a positive note: praise for de Beauvoir's intellectual integrity, her personal courage, and the continuing vitality of her concern for social issues. That she has constantly demonstrated a passionate commitment to ideals of freedom from want and oppression epitomizes all that is best in the tradition of western liberalism and is a source of inspiration, if not direction, to feminism.

─── Notes ──────────────────────────

INTRODUCTION

1 The history of feminism in France is documented in Macmillan 1981.
2 Rosalind Coward (1980) 'Are Women's Novels Feminist Novels?' *Feminist Review* 5: 53–64.
3 The debates on pornography have been widely documented in feminist journals. See, for a review of some of the issues, Deirdre English, Amber Hollibaugh, and Gayle Rubin (1982) 'Talking Sex: A Conversation on Sexuality and Feminism' *Feminist Review* 11: 40–52.
4 See Sara Ruddick, 'Maternal Thinking', and Nancy Chodorow and Susan Contratto, 'The Fantasy of the Perfect Mother', in Barrie Thorne and Marilyn Yalom (eds) (1982), *Re-thinking the Family: Some Feminist Questions* (New York: Longman): 76–94 and 54–75.

CHAPTER I

1 De Beauvoir has always been cited by feminists as one of the leading figures of feminism. Nevertheless, in her own country her work is problematic for the group known as *Psych et Po* who identify feminism as an 'heir of Western humanism' and a 'pillar of patriarchy in decline'. *Psych et Po* is avowedly

anti-feminist and committed to the development of what the group describes as a genuinely feminine language and politics. For a full account of the group's activities see Marks and Courtivron (1981): 31–3, 137–41, and Kaufmann–McCall.

2 Nor was Orwell alone in the portrayal of the sub-world of genteel poverty: Mrs Gaskell's *Cranford* and Barbara Pym's novels are peopled by individuals attempting to maintain their social status in conditions of financial hardship. Yet even given the decline in the de Beauvoirs' fortunes the distance – in material terms – between them and the majority of the French population at the time would still have been considerable.

3 Madsen (1977) gives an account of the relationship between de Beauvoir and Sartre, although the emphasis of the book may be regarded by some readers as a trifle romantic.

4 Quoted in Johnson (1981): 20. *Castor* (beaver) was Sartre's pet name for de Beauvoir.

5 Charlotte Brontë, *Jane Eyre* (London: Oxford University Press, 1961): 127.

6 Yet on some occasions Sartre could be extremely frank about his relationships with other women. For example, writing to de Beauvoir in 1948 he describes the time he spends with a young woman in terms that are both comic and dismissive. See LC, 342.

7 One other inequality in the relationship is that de Beauvoir appears to have provided rather more domestic services for Sartre than vice versa, although the extent of these services was never great since both lived for long periods in hotels. Nevertheless, Sartre's first recorded letter to de Beauvoir begins with a request to deposit his laundry at the cleaners (LC, 40).

8 The need for women to identify with male others has been most succinctly described in Miller (1979): 87–102.

9 The 'loss' of a sense of identity with a loved man seems to have provoked in other women besides de Beauvoir the same desire to write, or to write in a different way. For example, after the end of the marriage between Ted Hughes and Sylvia Plath, Plath's poetry took on a new, fierce voice and she produced what many critics argue is her finest work.

CHAPTER 2

1 The relationship between Sartre and Merleau-Ponty and the different political attitudes of each man are discussed in Hughes (1968): 153–226.

2 Works by Sartre: *Nausea*, London: Hamish Hamilton, 1962; *Intimacy*, *The Wall*, *The Room*, *Erostratus*, and *The Childhood of a Leader* published as *The Wall and Other Stories* (dedicated to Olga Kosakiewicz), New York: New Directions Publishing, 1975; *Sketch for a Theory of the Emotions*, London: Methuen, 1962; *Imagination*, Ann Arbor: The University of Michigan Press, 1962; *Being and Nothingness*, London: Methuen, 1969.

3 The term 'radical freedom' is used by de Beauvoir to describe her understanding of her situation in the years immediately after her graduation from the Sorbonne. She discusses her understanding of the term critically in PL, 15–17.

132 SIMONE DE BEAUVOIR

4 Quoted in Whitmarsh (1981): 70.
5 The pattern of traditional sexual jealousy to be found in *She Came to Stay* (a woman jealous of another woman's relationship with a man) is discussed by Toril Moi (1982).
6 De Beauvoir writes in the Preface, 'Here is the first of my books, and doubtless the only one, which you have not read before its publication. It is entirely concerned with you, and concerns you not at all', and concludes, 'Your death separates us. My death will not re-unite us' (CA).

CHAPTER 3

1 This view has most explicitly been stated by Pierre Zéphir (Zéphir 1982).
2 Throughout this book, references to *The Second Sex* are to the edition published by Bantam Books (Toronto) in 1964, in which the translation is by H. M. Parshley. Margaret Simons has recently argued that this translation seriously distorts de Beauvoir's views and arguments. This suggestion has been largely refuted by Deirdre Bair. See: Simons (1983) and Bair (1983).
3 This position is most fully and passionately articulated by Adrienne Rich, who in *Of Woman Born*, writes: 'To "mother" a child implies a continuing presence, lasting at least for nine months, more often for years. Motherhood is earned, first through an intense physical and psychic rite of passage – pregnancy and childbirth – then through learning to nurture, which does not come by instinct' (Rich 1979: 12).
4 For example, Virgina Woolf notes in her diary: 'Today Saturday the usual reasons have kept me recumbent' (*The Diary of Virginia Woolf, Volume I, 1915–1919*, New York and London: Harcourt Brace Jovanovich, 1977): 66.
5 See, for example, Mitchell (1975) and Sayers (1982).
6 Friedan wrote:
   'For women as well as men, education is and must be the matrix of human evolution. If today American women are finally breaking out of the housewife trap in search of new identity, it is quite simply because so many women have had a taste of higher education – unfinished, unfocused, but still powerful enough to force them on.' Betty Friedan, *The Feminine Mystique* (Harmondsworth: Penguin, 1983): 322.
7 The feminist literature on the relationship between sex and class inequality is now extensive. But for the most important contributions see: Barrett (1980), Delphy (1977), Zaretsky (1976), and Coward (1983).

CHAPTER 4

1 Among those who have written on capitalism and personal life are Herbert Marcuse (*Eros and Civilization*, Boston, Mass: The Beacon Press, 1955), Christopher Lasch (*The Culture of Narcissism*, New York: Norton, 1978), and David Riesman in his classic discussion of psychic loneliness in *The Lonely Crowd* (New Haven, Conn: Yale University Press, 1950).

2 For example, the campaign by women in nineteenth-century Britain to resist attempts by the state to define their sexuality have now been documented. See Walkowitz (1980).
3 George Eliot, *Middlemarch* (Harmondsworth: Penguin, 1966): 336.

CHAPTER 5

1 See the interview in *La Vie en Rose* (16 March 1984): 25–36.

CHAPTER 6

1 A list of the secondary literature is provided at the end of this book. Among books of note are: Jeanson (1966), Leighton (1975), and Marks (1973).
2 Jean-Paul Sartre in *Lettres au Castor*. Quoted in 'Simone de Beauvoir: Feministe', *La Vie en Rose* 16, March, 1984, p.37.
3 The issue of the relationship of Simone de Beauvoir to biology has been explored by Mary Lowenthal Felstiner (Felstiner 1980).
4 So great is the enthusiasm for de Beauvoir in North America that a Simone de Beauvoir Society now exists (c/o Yolanda Patterson, 440 La Mesa Drive, Menlo Park, California 94025, USA) and Concordia University (in Montreal, Canada) houses a Simone de Beauvoir Institute.

Bibliography

WORKS BY SIMONE DE BEAUVOIR,
CITED IN ORDER OF FIRST PUBLICATION.
ENGLISH EDITIONS REFERRED TO ARE
THOSE USED IN THIS TEXT

L'Invitée. Paris Gallimard, 1913.
   She Came to Stay. Harmondsworth: Penguin, 1966.
Pyrrhus et Cinéas. Paris: Gallimard, 1944.
Les Bouches inutiles (first performed in 1945).
Le Sang des autres. Paris: Gallimard,1945.
   The Blood of Others. Harmondsworth: Penguin, 1964.
Tous les hommes sont mortels. Paris: Gallimard, 1946.
   All Men Are Mortal. Cleveland: World Publishers, 1955.
Pour une morale de l'ambiguité. Paris: Gallimard, 1967.
   The Ethics of Ambiguity. New York: Philosophical Library, 1948.
L'Amérique au jour le jour. Paris: Morihien, 1948.
   America Day by Day. London: Duckworh, 1952.
Le Deuxième Sexe. Paris: Gallimard, 1949.
   The Second Sex. Toronto: Bantam Books, 1964.
Faut-il-brûler de Sade? *Les Temps Modernes*, December, 1951 and January, 1952.
   Must We Burn de Sade? London: Peter Nevill, 1953.
Les Mandarins. Paris: Gallimard, 1954.
   The Mandarins. London: Fontana, 1979.
Privilèges. Paris: Gallimard, 1955.

La Longue Marche. Paris: Gallimard, 1957.
   The Long March. London, André Deutsch, 1958.
Mémoires d'une jeune fille rangée. Paris: Gallimard, 1958.
   Memoirs of a Dutiful Daughter. Harmondsworth: Penguin, 1959.
Brigitte Bardot and the Lolita Syndrome. New York: Arno Publishing, 1960.
La Force de l'age. Paris: Gallimard, 1960.
   The Prime of Life. Harmondsworth: Penguin, 1962.
Djamila Boupacha. Paris: Gallimard, 1962.
   Djamila Boupacha. London: André Deutsch, 1962.
La Force des choses. Paris: Gallimard, 1963.
   Force of Circumstance. London: André Deutsch, and Weidenfeld & Nicolson, 1965.
Une Mort très douce. Paris: Gallimard, 1964.
   A Very Easy Death. Harmondsworth: Penguin, 1965.
Les Belles Images. Paris: Gallimard, 1966.
   Les Belles Images. London: Fontana, 1977.
La Femme rompue. Paris: Gallimard, 1967.
   The Woman Destroyed. London: Fontana, 1979.
La Vieillesse. Paris: Gallimard, 1970.
   Old Age. Harmondsworth: Penguin, 1978.
Tout compte fait. Paris: Gallimard, 1972.
   All Said and Done. Harmondsworth: Penguin, 1979.
Quand prime le spirituel. Paris: Gallimard, 1979.
   When Things of the Spirit Come First. London: Fontana, 1983.
La Cérémonie des adieux suivi de *Entretiens avec Jean-Paul Sartre*. Paris: Gallimard, 1981.
   Adieux: Farewell to Sartre. London: André Deutsch, 1984.
Lettres au Castor et à quelques autres, by Jean-Paul Sartre, ed. Simone de Beauvoir. Tome I: 1926–1939. Tome II: 1940–1963. Paris: Gallimard, 1983.

Secondary works on Simone de Beauvoir

Algren, Nelson (1965) The Question of Simone de Beauvoir. *Harpers* (May): 134–36.
Ascher, Carol (1981) *Simone de Beauvoir: A Life of Freedom*. Boston: The Beacon Press.
Bair, Deirdre (1983) In Summation: The Question of Conscious Feminism or Unconscious Misogyny in The Second Sex. *Simone de Beauvoir Studies* 1 (1): 56–67.
Bieber, Konrad (1979) *Simone de Beauvoir*. Boston: G. K. Hall.
Carter, Angela (1982) The Intellectual's Darby and Joan. *New Society* (28 January): 156–57.
Cottrell, Robert (1975) *Simone de Beauvoir*. New York: Frederick Ungar.
Cranston, Maurice (1978) Simone de Beauvoir. In J. Cruickshank (ed.) *The Novelist as Philosopher: Studies in French Fiction, 1935–1960*. Westport, Conn: Greenwood Press.

Cruickshank, John (1982) The Limitations of the Intellectual. *Times Higher Education Supplement* (26 February): 14.

Cunningham, John (1979) *The Second Sex* and Simone de Beauvoir. *Guardian* (24 July): 9.

Dijkstra, Sandra (1980) Simone de Beauvoir and Betty Friedan: The Politics of Omission. *Feminist Studies* 6 (2): 290–303.

Doeuff, Michele le (1980) Simone de Beauvoir and Existentialism. *Feminist Studies* 6 (2): 227–89.

Evans, Mary (1980) Views of Women and Men in the Work of Simone de Beauvoir. *Women's Studies International Quarterly* 3: 395–404.

—— (1983) Simone de Beauvoir: Dilemmas of a Feminist Radical. In Dale Spender (ed.) *Feminist Theorists*. London: The Women's Press.

Felstiner, Mary Lowenthal (1980) Seeing *The Second Sex* through the Second Wave. *Feminist Studies* 6 (2) (Summer): 249–76.

Fuchs, Jo-Ann (1980) Female Eroticism in *The Second Sex*. *Feminist Studies* 6 (2) (Summer): 304–13.

Gerassi, John (1976) Interview with Simone de Beauvoir. *Society* (January/February) 79–85.

Hardwick, Elizabeth (1953) The Subjection of Women. *Partisan Review* 20 (3) (May/June): 321–31.

Jardine, Alice (1979) Interview with Simone de Beauvoir. *Signs* 5 (2) (Winter): 224–36.

Jeanson, Francis (1966) *Simone de Beauvoir ou l'entreprise de vivre*. Paris: Editions du Seuil.

Johnson, Douglas (1981) La Grande Sartreuse. *London Review of Books* (15 October–4 November): 20–1.

Kaufmann-McCall, Dorothy (1979) Simone de Beauvoir, *The Second Sex* and Jean-Paul Sartre. *Signs* 5 (2) (Winter): 209–23.

Keefe, Terry (1983) *Simone de Beauvoir: Study of her Writings*. London: Harrap.

Leighton, Jean (1975) *Simone de Beauvoir on Women*. London: Associated University Presses.

Lloyd, Genevieve (1983) Masters, Slaves and Others. *Radical Philosophy* 34 (Summer): 2–9.

Madsen, Axel (1977) *Hearts and Minds: The Common Journey of Simone de Beauvoir and Jean-Paul Sartre*. New York: Morrow.

Marks, Elaine (1973) *Simone de Beauvoir: Encounter with Death*. New Brunswick, NJ: Rutgers University Press.

Moorehead, Caroline (1974) A Talk with Simone de Beauvoir. *New York Times Magazine* (2 June): 16–34.

O'Brien, Mary (1981) *The Politics of Reproduction*. London: Routledge & Kegan Paul.

Radford, C. B. (1965) The Authenticity of Simone de Beauvoir. *Nottingham French Studies* IV (2) (October): 91–104.

—— (1967–68) Simone de Beauvoir: Feminism's Friend or Foe? Part I. *Nottingham French Studies* VI (2) (October): 87–102; Part II. *Nottingham French Studies* VII (1) (May): 39–53.

Schwarzer, Alice (1984) *Simone de Beauvoir Today: Conversations 1972–1982*. London: Chatto & Windus, The Hogarth Press.

Simone de Beauvoir Society (1983) Simone de Beauvoir and Women. *Simone de Beauvoir Studies* 1 (1) (Fall).

Simons, Margaret A. (1983) The Silencing of Simone de Beauvoir: Guess What's Missing from *The Second Sex*. *Women's Studies International Forum* 6 (5): 559–64.

Simons, Margaret and Benjamin, J. (1979) Simone de Beauvoir: An Interview. *Feminist Studies* 5 (2) (Summer): 330–45.

Walters, Margaret (1976) The Rights and Wrongs of Women: Mary Wollstonecraft, Harriet Martineau and Simone de Beauvoir. In Ann Oakley and Juliet Mitchell (eds) *The Rights and Wrongs of Women*. Harmondsworth: Penguin.

Whitmarsh, Anne (1981) *Simone de Beauvoir and the Limits of Commitment*. Cambridge: Cambridge University Press.

Zéphir, Pierre (1982) *Le Néo-Feminisme de Simone de Beauvoir*. Paris: Denoel Gonthier.

OTHER WORKS REFERRED TO
OR CITED IN THE TEXT

Aronson, Ronald (1980) *Jean-Paul Sartre: Philosophy in the World*. London: George Allen & Unwin.

Barrett, Michele (1980) *Women's Oppression Today*. London: Verso.

Brenner, Johanna and Ramas, Maria (March/April 1984) Rethinking Women's Oppression. *New Left Review* 144.

Brombert, V. (1960) *The Intellectual Hero*. Philadelphia and New York: J. P. Lippincott.

Caws, Peter (1979) *Sartre*. London, Routledge & Kegan Paul.

Charlesworth, Max (1975) *The Existentialists and Jean-Paul Sartre*. Queensland: University of Queensland Press.

Chodorow, Nancy (1978) *The Reproduction of Mothering*. Berkeley: University of California Press.

Coward, Rosalind (1983) *Patriarchal Precedents: Sexuality and Social Relations*. London: Routledge & Kegan Paul.

Debray, Régis (1979) *Teachers, Writers, Celebrities: The Intellectuals of Modern France*. London: Verso.

Delphy, Christine (1977) *The Main Enemy*. London: Women's Research and Resources Centre Pamphlet.

Donohue, H. E. F. (1963) *Conversations with Nelson Algren*. New York: Hill & Wang.

Engels, Frederick (1967) *Origin of the Family, Private Property and the State*. Moscow: Foreign Languages Publishing House.

Gilligan, Carol (1983) *In a Different Voice*. Cambridge, Mass: Harvard University Press.

Goldmann, Lucien (1970) *Power and Humanism*. Nottingham: Bertrand Russell Peace Foundation.

Hughes, H. Stuart (1968) *The Obstructed Path: French Social Thought in the Years of Desperation, 1930–1960*. New York: Harper & Row.

Humphries, Jane (1981) Protective Legislation, the Capitalist State and Working Class Men: The Case of the 1842 Mines Regulation Act. *Feminist Review* 7: 1–33.

Johnson, R. W. (1981) *The Long March of the French Left*. London: Macmillan.

Kaplan, Cora (1979) Radical Feminism and Literature. *Red Letters* 9.

Kaufmann-McCall, Dorothy (1983) Politics of Difference: The Women's Movement in France from May 1968 to Mitterrand. *Signs* 9 (2): 282–93.

McIntosh, Mary (1978) Who Needs Prostitutes? The Ideology of Male Sexual Desire. In Carol Smart and Barry Smart (eds) *Women, Sexuality and Social Control*. London: Routledge & Kegan Paul.

Macmillan, James (1981) *Housewife or Harlot? The Place of Women in French Society, 1870–1940*. New York: St Martin's Press.

Marks, Elaine and Courtivron, Isabelle de (1981) *New French Feminisms*. Brighton: The Harvester Press.

Meszaros, Istvan (1979) *The Work of Sartre: Volume I, The Search for Freedom*. Brighton: The Harvester Press.

Miller, Jean Baker (1979) *Towards a New Psychology of Women*. Harmondsworth: Penguin.

Mitchell, Juliet (1975) *Psychoanalysis and Feminism*. Harmondsworth: Penguin.

Moi, Toril (1982) Jealousy and Sexual Difference. *Feminist Review* 11 (Summer): 53–68.

Plath, Sylvia (1982) *The Journals of Sylvia Plath*. New York: The Dial Press.

Rich, Adrienne (1979) *Of Woman Born*. London: Virago. First published 1976.

Sartre, Jean-Paul (1952) *The Communists and the Peace*. New York: Brasiller, 1968.

—— (1977) *Life/Situations: Essays Written and Spoken*. New York: Pantheon.

Sayers, Janet (1982) *Biological Politics*. London: Tavistock.

Shaktini, Namascar (1982) Displacing the Phallic Subject: Wittig's Lesbian Writing. *Signs* 8 (1) (Autumn): 29–44.

Signs (Autumn, 1981) Special Issue on French Feminist Theory. 7 (1).

Thompson, E. P. (1977) *Whigs and Hunters*. Harmondsworth: Peregrine.

Walkowitz, Judith (1980) *Prostitution and Victorian Society: Women, Class and the State*. Cambridge: Cambridge University Press.

Weeks, Jeffrey (1981) *Sex, Politics and Society*. London: Longman.

Zaretsky, Eli (1976) *Capitalism, the Family and Personal Life*. London: Pluto Press.

Name index

Thompson, E. P. 32, 113–14
Todd, O. 18
Tolstoy, Count L. 70, 92, 116

Walters, M. 124–25

Weeks, J. 105–06
Weil, S. 29
Whitmarsh, A. 49, 102–03
Woolf, V. 120

Zaza *see* Mabille

——— Subject index ———

Note: All references are to Simone de Beauvoir and her writings unless otherwise stated.

abortion xi, xii, 89, 101
'adventurer', ethics of 45
affluent society in novels 85–8
ageing 112–14
Algeria, x, 100–01, 103
All Men are Mortal 37, 46, 58, 79, 81, 96
All Said and Done 1, 71, 74, 91, 101, 107, 112, 118
America Day by Day 108–09, 111
animal life parallel 63–4
autobiographical works *see All Said and Done; Force of Circumstance; Memoirs of a Dutiful Daughter; Prime of Life; Very Easy Death, A*
autobiography in novels 27–8, 96
autonomy *see* independence

Belles Images, Les 79, 85–9
biological differences between sexes xvi, 61–6, 126–28
Blood of Others, The 103; equality of sexes 34; existentialism 35, 37, 79; middle class 6; setting of 27; story 46–7, 48, 58, 81, 95–6
bourgeois feminism xv–xvi
bourgeoisie *see* conventional life
Brigitte Bardot and Lolita Syndrome 105

calcium absorption 64–5
capitalism xiii; and aged 112–14; and personal relationships 87
career *see* women, working
Cérémonie des adieux, La 56
characters of men and women in books 58, 76–98, 116–17

childhood and early years 3–12, 123
children *see* motherhood
China 99, 106–07, 109
choice, personal, as matter of politics 103–04
class: structure and struggle 70, 72, 100, 125; working xiii–xv
commitment: political 29, 31; in relationships 79, 83
consciousness 35
constraints 34, 36, 42, 49, 89; *see also* conventional life; dependence
consumer society in novels 85–8
contraception xii, xv, 89
conventional life, rejected 2–6, 10, 13, 29–30, 34, 49, 59, 206, 121–23; *see also* constraints
cousin 11, 15, 29
critical discussions of work 121–29
Cuba 107–08

dangerous living 33
death 48; of friend 5, 12, 29, 54; of mother 8, 51–5
deceit 17, 19, 24, 43–4
dependence of women xiii, xvi–xvii, 16, 34, 59–60, 90–1, 112, 114; fear of 21; in novels 79, 82, 88, 95; *see also* constraints
despair, fiction of *see Belles Images, Les; Woman Destroyed, The*
Djamila Boupacha 103
domination, men's desire for 71–2, 76–7

education xv, 1, 3, 12; views on 31–2, 68–70, 89, 115
emancipation *see* independence
emotionalism 65
equality of sexes 34